More Light, Less Heat

Joseph Phelps

More Light, Less Heat

How Dialogue Can Transform
Christian Conflicts into Growth

Jossey-Bass Publishers
San Francisco

Jossey-Bass books and products are available through most bookstores. To contact Jossey-Bass directly, call (888) 378-2537, fax to (800) 605-2665, or visit our website at www.josseybass.com.

Substantial discounts on bulk quantities of Jossey-Bass books are available to corporations, professional associations, and other organizations. For details and discount information, contact the special sales department at Jossey-Bass.

For sales outside the United States, please contact your local Simon & Schuster International Office.

 Manufactured in the United States of America on Lyons Falls Turin Book. This paper is acid free and 100 percent totally chlorine free.

Library of Congress Cataloging-in-Publication Data

Phelps, Joseph, date.
  More light, less heat : how dialogue can transform Christian conflicts into growth / Joseph Phelps.
     p. cm.
  Includes bibliographical references and index.

  ISBN 0-7879-4286-3
  1. Conflict management—Religious aspects—Christianity. 2. Dialogue—Religious aspects—Christianity. 3. Church controversies. I. Title.
BV4597.53.C58 P594 1998
273'.9—ddc21

                                                                98-25321

FIRST EDITION
HB Printing   10 9 8 7 6 5 4 3 2 1

Contents

Preface

In 1994 I wrote a guest editorial for the local newspaper in which I took what I knew would be an unpopular position on a question being debated both in local churches and in public squares. At the end of the editorial, I invited the community to join me in substantive dialogue; there was still much to learn about the subject, and it desperately needed our collective wisdom.

The editorial received considerable public attention, but no one accepted the invitation to dialogue. Some offered to debate me in a public forum. Others offered to punch my lights out. Still others chose stealth communications: anonymous letters and angry phone calls. But not one person responded who was willing to join me in dialogue.

This experience began for me a personal quest for places where real, substantive dialogue was taking place. Surely they are out there, I reasoned, since the word "dialogue" appears so frequently in print. I interviewed pastors from across the theological spectrum. I talked to friends and associates from across the country. I put out notices in public places. After a while I began to feel like Abraham looking for a few good men: if not fifty, how about forty-five? Or twenty? Or ten? Thankfully, there were a few signs of people in dialogue. I celebrate them, and thank them for all they have taught me in this area. But overall, I became painfully aware that people, even

Christians, are not communicating much with each other in a sub-stantive way.

The scarcity of dialogue also led me to question exactly what I had in mind when I extended my invitation. Upon reflection, I wasn't sure what I meant by dialogue. It sounds nice, but what is it? I knew I wanted to stop the heated and acrimonious sound-bite wars that raged everywhere I turned, but I had no idea how to bring together the hurt and angry factions that exist in the church today.

I'm not alone. Many of us are tired of the fighting that takes place between Christians who disagree. We are weary and wary of rhetoric that substitutes for informed discussion. It is time for a new option.

More Light, Less Heat attempts to fill the void I found in my search for dialogue. It explores the "invisible line" that separates us from each other, and it calls the church to dialogue—a unique form of interaction that could transform the many conflicts surrounding our churches today into something good. Dialogue is defined and contrasted with other forms of interaction. Based on this definition, concrete examples and practical suggestions are offered to help both clergy and lay persons initiate and participate in this important work.

Having researched and written about dialogue, I must also acknowledge my own human limitations in putting it into practice. Like the apostle Paul, I have written more than I put into practice. (I am comforted by Paul's many compelling words on love, patience, and unity within the church, in contrast to his personal argument with Barnabas in Acts 15 over whether John Mark should accom-pany him on a missionary journey. "The disagreement became so sharp that they parted company" (15:39). So I stand in good com-pany.) Suffice it to say that knowing the skills necessary for healthy dialogue is but the beginning of the journey into a life of dialogue. My hope is that these chapters will provide the necessary equipment for other Christians like me to build up their weaker skills in this vital area.

Another irony is that, like most ministers, my ego beckons me to the front line of service, to be an action-oriented soldier in the army of the Lord. I aspire to feed the multitudes; to release the dams and let justice roll down like water; to defeat the enemy; to be, essentially, the hero. In some ways, dialogue feels like a digression or a demotion. Dialogue is not necessarily action-packed. To the contrary, at its best, dialogue is part of the everyday routine of life— as we hash out family rules, discuss a movie, or sit in a committee or denominational meeting. When it comes to dialogue, anxious activists can feel like young people who enlist in the army based on its exciting television commercials, only to find themselves chained to a mundane desk job.

And yet dialogue embodies the way of Jesus. It is loving, strong, intentional, risky, and redemptive. It is a tool of hope in the hands of Christians. Dialogue is active peacemaking at its most basic level. It is tedious only if one experiences everyday life as tedious, and on my better days I know it's not.

Granted, dialogue will not resolve all our differences. It does, however, give us a way to address them in the manner of our Lord. Ultimately, dialogue depends on a hope in Someone beyond ourselves. It is in this hope that this book is offered.

We begin by naming some of the many battlefields on which Christians fight each other for supremacy. Chapter 1 also enumerates a variety of responses to the catastrophes of these battles. Chapter 2 looks at dialogue as a distinct form of interaction for addressing our differences more constructively and clarifies how dialogue differs from other forms of communication. Chapter 3 provides motivations to entice conflicted Christians to consider dialogue instead of continued divisions. Here we begin to demonstrate models for dialogue. Chapter 4, the most practical, how-to part of the book, elaborates "Ten Guidelines for Dialogue" and offers examples of them in action. Chapter 5 slows down the presentation of dialogue in order to look at some specific challenges that face Christians who attempt to dialogue. Chapter 6 explores a particular way of framing conflicts through "polarity management" that I believe could be a significant tool for dialogue. Chapter 7 looks to the Bible for precedent and guidance in the field of dialogue. Chapter 8 tells the story of one church's efforts to wrestle creatively and constructively with a conflict by using tools of dialogue. Finally, Chapter 9 recognizes the many polarities in our world and celebrates dialogue as a hopeful way for Christians to transform the many conflicts in our world into something new.

I have a friend named Elton, one of the smartest and funniest people I know, who is forever coming up with unique observations about life. "Is that original?" I ask. "No," he answers, "I made it up."

Unfortunately, this book contains a great deal that is neither original nor made up by me. Fortunately, I have encountered many people over the last several years from across the country who helped me think about dialogue. My conversations with them formed the background from which this book has emerged. I wish I could recount the source of every idea. In any case, I hope I have tended their thoughts well and that those who recognize their ideas in these pages will be pleased.

My interest in dialogue was piqued in an Austin Presbyterian Seminary class taught by Terry Muck, who encouraged and pushed my thoughts along. Terry and the rest of the Austin Seminary community, particularly Prescott Williams, are some of the finest Christian teachers I have known. A grant from the Louisville Institute allowed me to further explore the question of dialogue. I thank the Institute for its dedication to the church's development.

My colleagues in ministry have been especially helpful both by challenging my thoughts and sharing their experiences. Mark Ashworth has been a constant friend and valued critic; many of the ideas here were honed during phone calls or long lunches with him. Larry Bethune and Kyle Childress have offered encouragement and wisdom at just the right time. They, along with a group of pastors known as the Neighborhood, provide a safe place for cultivating dreams and callings.

I have been blessed by two spiritual directors, Eileen Raffaniello in Austin, and Steve Wirth in Louisville. Both have been rich sources of insight for me by encouraging my law and grace sides to dialogue together in a happy, holy dance.

The three churches I have been honored to serve—Highland Park and Church of the Savior in Austin, and Highland in Louisville—have accepted my gifts, nurtured my weak areas, and given me far more than I have given them. They have shown me much about the importance of dialogue.

I have been enormously encouraged by a cadre of friends who encouraged my writing, including my former secretary, Myrna Jacks, and Don and Jo Ann Strickland. Walter McWhorter's technical assistance at the eleventh hour was most appreciated. My literary agent, Kathleen Neindorff, believed this project was worthy of publication and worked to make it happen. Editor Sarah Polster and staff have been truly outstanding.

Finally, I wish to thank my friend and wife, Terri, whose gentle questioning and careful editing of this work have made the final version much more readable than the original. I dedicate this book to her, my life dialogue partner, whose gifts of persistence, patience, and grace are a constant source of blessing.

JOSEPH PHELPS
Louisville, Kentucky
March, 1998

About the Author

Joseph Phelps is pastor of Highland Baptist Church in Louisville, Kentucky. He holds degrees from Southern Baptist Theological Seminary in Louisville (M. Div. 1978), and Austin Presbyterian Theological Seminary in Austin, Texas (D. Min. 1996). Before becoming pastor of Highland in 1997, he was the pastor of Church of the Savior, an American Baptist church in Austin, Texas, which he helped found in 1985.

Phelps spent two years interviewing Christians from across the theological spectrum on their experiences in dialogue as part of a research project for the Louisville Institute for the Study of Religion in America. His experiences during various culture wars in his community, as well as during the fundamentalist takeover of the Southern Baptist Convention, make him a veteran of the conflicts that call for dialogue.

Phelps has been a community leader in starting a food bank, a soup kitchen, a community ministry, and anti-violence campaigns. He was a weekly newspaper columnist in Austin for eight years.

Phelps and his wife, Terri, have four children.

God,
good beyond all that is good,
fair beyond all that is fair,
in you is calmness
peace
and concord.

Heal the dissensions
that divide us from one another
and bring us back to a unity of love
bearing some likeness
to your divine nature.

Amen.

—Dionysius of Alexandria
(A.D. 264)

The Heat of Our Battles

In a rural county in Kentucky, a church's annual report to the area Baptist office caused a firestorm when someone noticed that under the category "other ordained ministers in your congregation" the church had listed the new pastor's wife, a pastoral counselor who had been ordained to ministry some years earlier by a church in another state. Fundamentalist leaders in area churches took the inclusion of her name in the report as an affront to their conviction that women should not be ordained. They met together to plan an attack both on the church and the woman, who worked as a counselor in a neighboring county.

The pastor learned of the plans to remove his church from the Baptist association and sought a meeting with the disgruntled pastors. They refused to talk with him or to meet his wife and learn of their ministry, stating that there was nothing they could do to work together, given the pastor and his wife's invalid interpretation of scripture. They told him that to discuss the issue would be to compromise their beliefs.

"What if an ordained woman like my wife presented herself for membership in your church?" the pastor asked theoretically. "Would you accept her?"

"Absolutely not," they quickly answered.

. . . .

In Chicago, the pastor of a Presbyterian church established an "information hall" in the vestibule outside the sanctuary of his 600-member suburban church. Believing that all sides should be heard and that "an informed congregation is a prepared congregation," the pastor encouraged committees and groups represented in the church, as well as members working in other organizations, to set up tables to display the activities in which they were involved and offer literature to interested members.

Reservations for the tables quickly filled up. Church ministry committees had tables presenting upcoming events in the life of the church. Several local counseling centers asked for tables, as did the community ministries program and the local peace and justice coalition.

From there things got interesting. The table sponsored by the local presbytery was placed near another table promoting a new, unofficial denominational magazine that represented the conservative wing of Presbyterians. Promise Keepers also had a table. So did the local Women in Ministry group. Both sides of the local airport issue were there, as were both sides of the abortion issue. A vocal group opposing school board policies also had a table.

By the time the call to worship was given on the first Sunday of the information hall, the tension could be felt in the air. Harsh words had been exchanged in the previous hour between representatives at the tables. Certain members were infuriated that groups they opposed had been granted permission to display materials in their church. There were five scribbled messages taped to the pastor's door asking to meet with him immediately. One leading member, a professor in women's studies at the university, refused to shake the pastor's hand. "How could you betray us like this?" she asked. "Those fundamentalist Neanderthals are pushing the worst kind of propaganda on our people. Let me know when they're gone. Then I'll think about coming back."

• • • • • • •

When the International Bible Society (IBS) announced plans to publish a "gender-accurate" version of the Bible, the announcement met with strong and immediate resistance from the conservative wing of the already-conservative evangelical wing of the church. Opponents labeled the proposed publication a "unisex" version of the Bible and publicly portrayed it as part of a "feminist ideology." They quickly mobilized groups with economic clout to force the cancellation of the project.

Ron Sider, also an evangelical, responded, "This deliberate use of false and misleading innuendo is hardly an honest, fair way to debate important issues within the Christian community." Nonetheless, as criticism mounted from powerful groups like the Southern Baptist Sunday School Board, conservative seminary presidents, and James Dobson's Focus on the Family, the IBS announced they were dropping all plans for the new translation. Sider, in an open letter, expressed disappointment at the haste with which the complex issue of the legitimacy of a new Bible version was addressed. "That [IBS] would allow an ad hoc, one-sided (though admittedly powerful) group to dictate their publishing decisions is extremely disturbing. . . . How could the IBS reverse its decision . . . without widespread consultation with the full range of evangelical scholars?" ("'Economic Hardball' . . .," 1998).

• • • • • • •

The church needs to talk about its talking, or the lack thereof. Mostly, we fight and yell. We lob verbal hand grenades, often in battles that reflect the tactics of a larger cultural division, sometimes called culture war, among us. We do lots of speaking, but little talking. Speaking is monological, the act of one person verbalizing a thought or a word. Talking is dialogical; it requires at least two active participants who engage in speaking as well as listening. We learn to speak at a young age, but learning to talk is a lifelong pursuit.

The air is filled with speeches about the current culture war among Christians in U.S. churches over topics such as abortion, the role of women in church life, welfare reform, censorship, gun control, affirmative action, homosexuality, and euthanasia. Highly visible and well-financed organizations bombard us from all sides with positions on these topics, lobbying churches and individuals to take their side.

Within local churches, other skirmishes flare up. Some reflect battles within the larger culture war going on across the country between traditionalists and progressives over the values and rules, spoken and unspoken, by which we will live together. Other church battles originate from conflict unique to a particular church. Sources of local conflict can be virtually anything: differing tastes in worship styles, comfort levels with evangelistic strategies, attitudes toward including new members who are different from long-time members, the way the church uses and governs its finances, identification with the church's denomination, the way the church relates to competing groups within the denomination, the amount of authority given to a pastor, the decision to relocate the church, use of church facilities by outside groups. . . . The list is endless. Like the human body in which cells multiply by splitting, it seems that the church's most visible public attribute is its ability to divide over issues from the basic to the trivial.

Author Richard Foster, lamenting the myopic nature of the church, recalls the following story.

> I was walking in San Francisco along the Golden Gate bridge when I saw a man about to jump off. I tried to dissuade him from committing suicide and told him simply that God loved him. A tear came to his eye. I then asked him, "Are you a Christian or a Jew or a Hindu, or what?"
> He said, "I am a Christian."
> I said, "Me too. Protestant or Catholic?"
> "Protestant."

"Me too," I said. "What denomination?"

"Northern Baptist," he said.

"Well, me too," I said. "That's amazing. What a small world. Northern Conservative Baptist or Northern Liberal Baptist?"

"Northern Conservative Baptist," he answered.

I said, "I don't believe it. What are the chances of that? Me too! Northern Conservative Fundamentalist Baptist or Northern Conservative Reformed Baptist?"

"Northern Conservative Fundamentalist Baptist."

"Remarkable!" I said. "Northern Conservative Fundamentalist Baptist Great Lakes Region or Northern Conservative Fundamentalist Baptist Eastern Region?"

"Northern Conservative Fundamentalist Baptist Great Lakes Region."

I said, "It's a miracle! Northern Conservative Fundamentalist Baptist Great Lakes Region of 1879 or Northern Conservative Fundamentalist Baptist Great Lakes Region of 1912?"

"Northern Conservative Fundamentalist Baptist Great Lakes Region of 1912," he answered.

"Die, heretic," I said, and pushed him off the bridge.

Some have tried to put a positive spin on the church's conflicts and splits. They suggest that, like human cells, the church's splits eventually help it grow and permeate our culture. Maybe so, but if this is a good thing, then why is it so often painful and destructive to individuals as well as to the church's witness? Could it be that this splitting and multiplying from our conflicts create *cancerous* cells instead of healthy, vibrant ones?

Something is clearly wrong. Disagreements are magnified into major conflicts worthy of extreme tactics. Believing that "all's fair in love and war," Christian people misrepresent each other's positions.

They demonize those who disagree with them, fulfilling an important maxim of war: have a clearly identified enemy. In the heat of battle, enemies are defined as "all who disagree with our side." It is easy to see that the current manifestations of our Christian culture war encourage the misuse of power. (For a fuller treatment of the misuse of power in our culture war, see Hunter, 1994, especially p. 221ff.)

The result is confusing and frightening for many of us. For example, when someone like conservative leader James Dobson contends that "[t]he heated dispute over values in Western nations is simply a continuation of the age-old struggle between the principles of righteousness and kingdom of darkness" (1995, p. 28), I am personally not sure what to make of such a statement. Dobson may be shooting at people far more to the Left than I am, but as he is firing away, his rifle is pointed in my direction, which is clearly to the Left of him, and the bullets are whizzing over my head!

The effects of the church's high-profile fighting have been costly and ugly, as Tom Sine reports in *Cease Fire! Searching for America's Culture Wars* (1995). It has sapped our strength from the real work of love to which Christ calls us. It has marred the church's witness to the world. It has stained our souls as we have fostered resentments toward others. Fellow Christians have been wounded or driven out of service. Still others, upon seeing the spiritual violence, have retreated from church involvement, never to return.

In military double-speak, human casualties of war are referred to as "collateral damage." It is imperative that participants in the church's battles remember this: collateral damage is people—relationships, lives, and livelihoods.

"Don't Shoot 'Til You See the Whites of Their Eyes"

If these battlefield images sound exaggerated, it is because the culture war is a heated, wide-ranging battle of words and ideas, rather than one that threatens us physically. There are, of course, tragic examples of a culture war becoming physically violent, such as when an abortion opponent murdered a Florida doctor who performed abortions. More frequent examples can be cited in countries such as Iraq and Bosnia, where religious and political conflicts too often result in physical violence.

Generally, in the United States, the culture war is more clandestine; it moves from one front to the next with ease and is only rarely identified by the name "culture war." Thus, it is hard to pinpoint with any accuracy. Like westerners trying to understand the recent wars in Bosnia and Croatia, or between Israel and Palestine, without knowing these cultures' histories and the subtle nuances of the competing sides, most casual observers of the Christian manifestation of culture war witness the animosity it elicits and scratch their heads. "Why can't we all just get along?" they ask, echoing Rodney King's now-famous line following the Los Angeles riots.

Culture war battles take place in most major institutions of our country: universities, public elementary and secondary schools, businesses, national and local politics, and, of course, within the major religions. For example, in Austin, Texas, the culture war has erupted recently on several fronts. It broke out at the University of Texas in heated debates over whether courses in multiculturalism should be required for all students and over competing interpretations of American and Texas history. It created division at the local school board over the use of Pumsy, a puppet used to teach values and self-esteem in the elementary schools, and over the appropriateness of Maya Angelou's *I Know Why the Caged Bird Sings* as literature for high school English classes. It divided the community over whether tax abatements awarded to Apple Computer should be rescinded when it was discovered that the company offered health insurance for same-sex partners. These battles over our culture even threatened the morning routine of my family, as Congress argued over the efficacy of public television, which broadcasts *Sesame Street* and *Barney and Friends*.

This culture war belongs to no one in particular. No specific groups can be blamed for or take credit for waging this war. It is not a concerted strategy being deployed. Nor should it be identified too closely with the inflammatory rhetoric of marginal militant politicians such as Patrick Buchanan, who contended in a 1992 speech to the Republican National Convention that "we are engaged in a war for the nation's soul," or the goading, "I-dare-you" style of radio personality Rush Limbaugh, or their counterparts on the other side of the debate. These public figures serve in a sense as caricatures—exaggerated examples of the larger but less visible, less specific struggle that shapes a great many of the battles in which so many bystanders are pinned down in the crossfire.

The culture war has also created new divisions between the community of churches as well as within individual churches. I say *new* divisions because, as James Davison Hunter (1991) demonstrates, it has complicated old lines of division and created new allies and new enemies. Sociologists such as Hunter and Robert Wuthnow have noted that it is less informative to classify people or churches by their denomination (Catholic, Protestant, Jewish, other, nonreligious) than by whether they are "progressive" or "orthodox," Hunter's terms for liberal and conservative, or Left and Right (1991, p. 42ff; see also Wuthnow 1989).

Christian Responses to Conflict

The many forms of battle among Christians elicit varied responses. The most visible response is the queuing of soldiers on both sides of an issue to go into battle. Some have voluntarily joined the battle out of such deeply held convictions that there is no room for the existence of the other side within the Christian faith. They enter the battle confident that God is with them on the side of truth.

Other soldiers are draftees—pastors and lay leaders caught up in the fray, like bystanders in a barroom brawl in a western movie.

There is no time to explore the issues in depth, to ask questions, or to weigh the nuances of all the arguments. Don't think, fight! Figure out which side you are on, and start slugging the enemy!

The opposite response to the fighters is the approach of the lovers. This group refuses to acknowledge any legitimate disputes among Christians, preferring that we not talk about divisive issues in order to maintain a "polite pluralism" among us. The lover approach is embraced by some Christians with the best of intentions on behalf of the work of the church. They honestly believe that Christians should not argue or fight. Others, however, adopt this response as a cowardly or lazy way to avoid the discomfort of conflict. In either case, this approach tries to deny the seriousness of the conflict among us. Both are draft dodgers in the Christian culture war.

Yet another response is to avoid the fight by associating only with like-minded Christians. In some cases this insulation from adversaries is not intentional, but the result of the limited circles in which these Christians run. These folk aren't aware of the larger spectrum within the Christian community because no one they know differs significantly from them.

Finally, there are those who acknowledge the various positions within the church's many conflicts, but deny that these differences are worth fighting about. "You believe what you think is right, and I'll believe what I think is right, and that's okay." This relativism in the name of peace honors neither the position of the adversary nor one's own position.

The Option of Dialogue

There is yet another path through the Christian culture war besides fighting or walking away from the fight. It is a difficult and sometimes lonely road where the spotlight rarely shines. It calls for a different kind of courage from that of the fighter and a different kind of love from that of the pacifist. It is the way of dialogue.

Dialogue is more than a form of communication. It is a way of thinking, seeing, hearing, relating to, and, of course, talking with our "enemies." It is a multifaceted, interdisciplinary process that touches on diverse and complex fields: psychology (human patterns, fears, prejudices), philosophy (how do we "know"?), sociology (group dynamics, the role of culture), politics (rhetoric, use of power), communication theory, and ethics, to name a few. When dialogue is entered into by Christians, we add yet one more field to the interdisciplinary mix: theology (who is God, what is God's will, what is evil, how do God's people relate to enemies?). To say the least, it is a complicated endeavor, which may be why dialogue is such a rarity.

Interestingly, the *idea* of dialogue is popular among Christian leaders today, although it is not always referred to by the term "dialogue." Most observers of the tragedies resulting from the church's inability to deal with its polarities call for the sides in dispute to engage in better conversation. This call for dialogue is heard from across the spectrum.

Richard Neuhaus, editor of the conservative journal *First Things*, writes, "Our quarrel with politicized fundamentalism is not so much over the form of religion's role in society but over the substance of the claim made. To put it differently, our quarrel is primarily theological. Unless that quarrel is transformed into an engagement that moves toward dialogue, we will continue to collaborate, knowingly or not, in discrediting the public responsibility of religion" (1984, p. 19). Conservative Bill Bennett suggests, "[W]here liberals and conservatives can find common ground—we should. Where we cannot, we should engage in robust, spirited, civilized debate. But people of goodwill should not allow this vital national debate to be sidetracked by mudslingers" (1994, 10).

Os Guinness, conservative sociologist and Christian author, calls for a "chartered pluralism" and a "respect for people, truth, the common good, and the American constitutional tradition," for "principled participation," and "principled persuasion" (quoted in Sire 1993,

p. 51). Guinness led in the writing of the *Williamsburg Charter*, a document on the First Amendment's religious liberty clause, signed by nearly 200 national leaders in 1988. It proposes "how we should contend with each other's deepest differences in the public sphere. It is a call to a vision of public life that will allow conflict to lead to consensus, religious commitment to reinforce political civility. In this way, diversity is not a point of weakness but a source of strength." (Hunter and Guinness, 1990, 128). It contends that "the issue is not only what we debate, but *how*" (133, italics added).

From the progressive evangelical movement comes a similar call from *Sojourners* editor Jim Wallis:

> Religious faith must not become another casualty of the culture wars. Indeed, religious communities should be the ones calling for a cease-fire. . . . Name-calling is no substitute for real and prayerful dialogue between different constituencies with conflicting priorities. . . . The American people are disgusted with politics as usual and hungry for political vision with spiritual values that transcend the old and failed categories that still imprison public discourse and stifle our creativity. The religious community could help lead that discussion and action toward new political alternatives. Toward that end, we need a new dialogue with all sectors of the religious community (1994, p. 18).

Wallis helped orchestrate a document entitled "The Cry for Renewal" (1995), which was endorsed by a wide array of religious leaders from across the country, including Joan Brown Campbell, General Secretary of the National Council of Churches; conservative theologian J. I. Packer; James Forbes, pastor of Riverside Church in New York; and Milton Efthimiou of the Greek Orthodox Church. It advocates, "Let a new dialogue begin at national, regional, and local levels around the country. Let politicized religion be replaced with prophetic faith to forge new coalitions of Christian conscience across the land" ("Cry for Renewal," 1995).

Another progressive evangelical author, Tom Sine, agrees: "Isn't it time for those who are advocates of a more inclusive, tolerant society to reach out to more conservative Christians with whom they may disagree on political issues? Isn't it time for progressive Christians to sit down at table with their more conservative sisters and brothers and rediscover the faith that unites them?" (1995, p. 45).

Further to the Left, historian and author Martin Marty laments, "What we have now in America [in our culture war] is an argument. A conversation is different. It's not guided by the answers. It's guided by the questions" (1995b, p. 3G).

From the Left, process theologian John Cobb makes a proposal: "Representatives of the several theologies [regarding a Christian response to world religions] need to dialogue openly with one another, not with the goal of finding something in common, or of defeating each other in debate, but with the goal that each will be challenged by the insights of the other so that a new consensus can emerge that does justice to the basic commitment of all" (1994, p. 750). Toward that end, Gabriel Fackre calls for scholarly critics-in-residence from both evangelical and ecumenical sides to "become acquainted with one another." These relationships would reveal the pitfalls and blessings that lie ahead when making course corrections that take a group into areas previously traveled by their counterparts. Although Fackre admits that "[a]ll this may be too much to hope for in our tribalist era," he still contends that "[i]t is time for would-be reformers to come together for what Luther called 'mutual conversation and consolation,' as well as for mutual correction" (1993, p. 1169).

Swords into Plowshares

People are fed up with the way the conflicts among Christians have been handled by those who purport to speak for groups within the church. It is time to decentralize the conversation, to enable grass-roots Christians to dialogue with one another in communities across the land.

Clearly absent in the various calls for dialogue is a recognition of the need for tools and skills necessary for Christians at the grass-roots level to transform fighting into talking. We hear the challenge to beat swords into plowshares, but these beautiful words fall on deaf ears. Many of us don't even know what a plowshare looks like, much less how to make one and use it! Our leaders are not engaged in the kind of interaction that they call for, so how can we be expected to begin? We lack sufficient models for dialogue.

The presentation of dialogue in this book is designed primarily for grassroots Christians who are tired of the animosity and rhetoric of the Christian brand of culture war. It is a primer for people who want to find a way to call a cease-fire. The only way we will halt the divisiveness of our present conflict is by involving Christians at all levels, especially the local level, in dialogue with each other about the issues that matter. Only when the ideological issues that divide the church are given a face, only when people with the basic skills of dialogue are talking to their family members, friends, coworkers, and neighbors who are on opposite sides in these battles over val-ues and truth, only then can we hope to break the impasse that has our churches pinned down in the crossfire.

But be prepared. The outcome of dialogue between embattled Christians may surprise you. It may well be that even if we engage in Spirit-infused dialogue, even if we are honest and courageous, even if all goes as it should, the battle between two distinct sides may continue creating uncomfortable tension within the church. Perhaps this tension is necessary, even normative, as long as we live on this side of Glory. If this is true, dialogue will not resolve the ten-sion, but it will allow the tension to be transformed into the work of God.

2

The Light of Dialogue

"So, let's get talking! Why waste time and energy dissecting the term 'dialogue'? We know how to talk. If talking is what we need to do, let's get to it."

As a person prone to dispense with the preliminaries, such as reading instructions before beginning assembly, I understand this sentiment. Doubtless, there are some within the Christian community who are adequately equipped to advance to the talking stage of dialogue with adversaries. Some of us, however, need help in preparing for dialogue, lest we thwart the process before it even begins. A primer on dialogue is necessary for a number of reasons:

- Though we're bombarded with words, few of us know about careful listening and speaking. The dominant communication pattern among people who disagree on church issues is monologue, not dialogue. Sometimes we share the floor with others, but only if they agree with us. As one conservative admitted, "We only associate with like-minded people, so the more we hear and confirm each other's views, the more certain we are that those views are right. We're all sort of in our own self-imposed ghettos, in our own little clusters. We don't really know what's out there." Careful listening and speaking in such a safe, self-justifying context is unnecessary.

- Most people are naturally defensive. We instinctively protect ourselves. When an object comes quickly toward our faces, our hands reflexively go up in defense; the same thing happens when someone challenges our beliefs or actions. Our emotional defenses go up in a reflex response, closing off our ability to hear with openness and flexibility. This pattern is so ingrained, so instinctive, that we revert to it despite our best intentions and often without our awareness.

- We have a "limited tolerance of dissent" (Kelly, n.d.). After pledging to be open in dialogue, we soon find ourselves passing our threshold for listening patiently to those we disagree with. We give in to our impulses to correct and explain. Once we have done so, we then wish to see the problem resolved. However, points of disagreement in dialogue are more likely to be illuminated than they are to be resolved. This reality can be a source of frustration because we live in a culture that is accustomed to quick fixes.

- Disagreements about religion, especially with those we live close to, is a particularly sensitive and volatile subject. The deeper our devotion to our faith, the more easily offended we can be by our neighbor's differing beliefs. Differing and conflicting beliefs can threaten us, for we assume that the presence of another view calls into question the correctness or adequacy of our views. When threatened, our defenses rise and dialogue stops.

It is interesting to observe how much easier it is for Christians to converse with someone from an entirely different religious tradition than with a Christian whose beliefs differ from ours. For example, it is easier for a Baptist pastor to converse with a Jewish rabbi than it is for a Baptist pastor from the Left to talk with a Baptist pastor on the Right. The rabbi is theologically and relationally a safe distance from the Baptist pastor, and the conversation is often easy, genuinely inquisitive, and bathed in civility. On the other hand, a conversation between Baptists from different sides of the conflicts of the last decade will likely be strained, guarded, and brief. It is simply too close for comfort.

- Many people wear deep scars from past emotional wounds inflicted by their religious adversaries. These experiences are difficult to forget or overlook. Resentment is natural, but it is an impediment to dialogue.

These various impediments to dialogue illustrate why it will be helpful for Christians to explore the nature of dialogue. We need to make sure that when we say "dialogue" we are all talking about the same thing. Otherwise, we may enter into a process only to find ourselves hurt and disappointed again. With some pre-dialogue exploration of the issue, genuine growth—intellectual, spiritual, emotional, and relational—is more likely to occur.

Perceptions of Dialogue

The word "dialogue" conjures up a variety of mental pictures, depending on one's life experiences. For example, dialogue can be understood as debating one's adversary in an intense, time-consuming, emotionally draining power struggle. Most of us avoid this kind of confrontation, having found it to be fruitless and polarizing. (We will explore the difference between dialogue and debate later in this chapter. Suffice it for now to say that debate, even civil debate, is not the same as dialogue.)

Others see dialogue as a call to civility: to diffuse anger, speak kindly to an adversary, and attempt to bury the hatchet by avoiding issues that divide us. Such was the case when two pastors with conflicting convictions were asked to co-officiate at a funeral. Given the context, there was an unspoken agreement to avoid divisive issues and to engage in polite conversation about noncontroversial issues: traffic, weather, church attendance, building programs. When the funeral was over, the two pastors congratulated each other on how well they had talked to each other. In retrospect, while this may have been the appropriate form of interaction given the setting, it does not constitute what we will define as dialogue.

Still others understand dialogue as an attempt to negotiate a compromise, to find a good meeting point between conflicting views, and to agree to settle for the lowest common denominator. Compromise can be a legitimate, albeit usually temporary, strategy in making such decisions as where to locate a denominational headquarters or what musical styles a congregation should use. But it can be little more than an evasion tactic when proposed by someone who simply wants everyone to "just get along." In either case, this is not the same thing as dialogue.

Some simply recoil at the term "dialogue" because it sounds so "p. c." (politically correct). If you find yourself feeling resistant to the term "dialogue," try substituting the word "conversation" in its place, at least temporarily. "Conversation" is a more general term, but close enough in meaning, and not nearly as loaded as the term "dialogue." I have retained the term "dialogue" because it denotes a method of interaction that, while lacking a universal definition, is nonetheless distinct from other methods. We will now explore the distinct elements of dialogue and propose a definition that emerges from them for our use in the many places where the church needs deeper, more thoughtful interaction.

Dialogue's Legacy

Socrates (421 B.C.) reveals an early understanding of dialogue as a particular form of communication. The great philosopher came upon dialogue almost by accident when the oracle of Delphi declared that there was no one alive wiser than Socrates. Socrates, knowing his own limitations, set out to prove the oracle wrong. He went about questioning others in such a way as to help them to see truths and falsehoods, probing and prodding them to go deeper into the insights and discoveries that they themselves possessed, thus uncovering their own true wisdom. Whether Socrates found someone wiser than himself is unknown, but he is credited with originating the process that became known as the dialogical method of communication.

Plato, Socrates' student, developed this method as an alternative to the prevalent teaching method of his day—the lecture. Plato accused lecturers of charging money to teach people opinions packaged as wisdom. In place of the lecture, Plato taught by using interaction and a participatory method of learning. Dialogue partners participated on an equal footing and tried to help expand each other's thoughts with both argument and encouragement, creating a kind of "intellectual midwifery" that gave birth to something new and valid in the pursuit of the truth (Pieterse, 1990, pp. 227–228).

In Socrates' and Plato's methods we see key elements of dialogue as we will define it for our use: the coming together of persons who desire to learn and grow in the truth through building on the insights and observations of others, particularly adversaries.

Teamwork

The term "dialogue" comes from the Greek "dialogos" (*dia* = through, *logos* = word). The literal translation suggests its meaning: the use of words moving people in conversation through an interaction to a place where new meaning is uncovered. In dialogue, speech moves beyond either simple interaction or competitive exchange to an activity in which participants work together as a team. Martin Buber, whose well-known reflections on the "I-Thou" nature of interaction between humans and the Holy One are foundational to the understanding of dialogue, believed the key to genuine dialogue was turning to the other in order to establish "a living mutual relation" between the two (1965, p. 19). Personal convictions and assumptions are offered to the enterprise of dialogue as resources or tools to be used by the entire team of dialogue participants, of which the individual is a part. This approach allows dialogue participants to observe the various thought processes at work within the dialogue topic and to test their own convictions on the anvil of the dialogue, with the hope that more light and truth will come forth.

This hope that dialogue can produce something new and fresh was attested to in the following conversation between psychotherapist Carl Rogers and anthropologist Gregory Bateson on their way to a public dialogue. The moderator for the evening asked Bateson, "How will I know whether or not we have done our job tonight?" Bateson responded, "If either Carl or I say something that we haven't said before, we'll know that it's a success" (quoted in Anderson, 1994, p. 10).

The teamwork of dialogue moves the conversation away from win/lose, either/or. At least for the duration of the dialogue, adversaries become allies, working together to break new ground. It is a temporary truce from fighting. Objections will still be raised; disagreement based on non-negotiable convictions will still hold firm; but the tone is different. The goal is changed from conquering to growing, from silencing to knowing, from telling to asking. Questions are employed as tools for probing, not weapons for stabbing. New possibilities are considered (Tracy, 1987, p. 21). We dialogue "so that creativity can be liberated" (Bohm, 1991, p. 82).

Other hopeful, constructive possibilities emerge when dialogue is framed in a spirit of teamwork. When personal views on the dialogue topic are offered to the team, there is a better possibility that assumptions and convictions can be viewed more objectively by both the team and the individual, allowing participants to see both points of incoherence as well as points of insight in their own and others' positions.

Incoherence is more than illogical thought; it is a line of thinking that may produce undesired consequences. In the abortion conflict, for example, most pro-life advocates do not want their conviction to mean that low-income women who decide to abort will be forced to obtain medically dangerous abortions, nor do they want to see children raised by parents who do not want them. Similarly, most pro-choice advocates do not want their position to result in abortions being casually used as a form of birth control. In dialogue, new implications of a position may be uncovered that will cause the position to be re-examined for coherence and desired outcome. Thus, the dialogue sends participants deeper into themselves in order to explore their own positions and their implications more carefully.

As dialogue progresses, participants grow to see their adversaries as "colleagues with different views" (Senge, 1990, p. 245). Such a recognition diffuses the feelings of anger or vulnerability that often accompany dialogue. Participants can also see how much of their thoughts are not original to them, but have come from "the pool of culturally acceptable assumptions" (p. 242). In the process, dialogue becomes less threatening, for all participants are invited to offer their thoughts in a spirit of openness as a contribution to the work at hand.

This, of course, requires an increasingly higher level of humility and grace toward our dialogue partners. For genuine dialogue to transpire, we must be willing to grant that our adversaries honestly believe the positions they espouse, even if we think that their positions are wrong. As Stephen Carter laments, "For too many of us who are deeply committed to our beliefs, all the integrity is on one side: our side. The other side doesn't have any. (If they did they would agree with us.)" (1996, p. 26).

Sadly, current church battles move the church in the opposite direction from teamwork. To curb the increasing polarization between the two sides, some propose that the church stop using the term "culture wars" because it suggests an "us-versus-them" mentality that has many damaging effects, not the least of which is the harm it does to the possibility of conversation (Woodbridge, 1995, p. 22; Williams, 1997). If the enemy is demonized, then the call for dialogue is vilified and rejected, and an important resource for the healing of the church is lost.

Trust

A second element in dialogue is trust. There must be trust at three levels—trust in one's own position, trust in the other participants in the dialogue, and trust in the process of dialogue itself. If there is a lack of trust in any one of these three elements, dialogue will shut down, or more likely, mutate into another form of interaction, usually a negative one.

Trust begins with self-trust—a comfort and conviction in one's position. Dialogue can be entered into only by those "familiar enough and confident enough about [their] faith that it can be risked in disclosure and vulnerability" (Brueggemann, 1994, p. 19). Self-trust can also refer to a confidence in one's basic personal worth or position as a human being that transcends the correctness of the position he or she holds. This trust is essentially an inner strength, or we may say, a basic trust in God who grants all people worth regardless of the coherence of their convictions on a given issue.

Here we must be frank and self-evaluating: if self-trust is necessary for dialogue, then it may well be that dialogue is not for everyone, for few possess the inner peace that is the evidence of self-trust. Without self-trust, the questions and challenges posed by the adversary will create suspicion and defensiveness in ill-equipped participants. The result may be a larger conflict than the one that was the subject of the dialogue.

The second form of trust, trust in the dialogue partner, is also necessary in order to handle the utter openness before one's adversary that is required in dialogue. Few of us have experienced this position of vulnerability to any great degree, and fewer still are prepared for it. It is a new and startling experience, perhaps related to

Jesus' call to His followers to lose one's life in order to find it. In the process of dialogue, participants "lose" the safety of their carefully crafted defenses and academic diplomas in order to expose themselves and their ideas to the scrutiny of both self and the other, and pledge to walk with the other through a similar process. Dialogue requires "the willingness to play with new ideas, to examine them and test them. As soon as we become overly concerned with 'who said what,' or 'not saying something stupid,' the playfulness will evaporate" (Senge, 1990, p. 246).

There is risk here. A trusting person can be exploited in dialogue. Words can be misinterpreted. Confidences can be betrayed. Exploration of new thoughts can be misinterpreted as a sign of weakness or doubt (by both adversaries *and* allies). Openness to questions may take participants into unexplored, uncharted territories where they lose a sense of control. Exposing one's thoughts to the scrutiny of the group may reveal mistakes in logic or convictions. This can be embarrassing, like the embarrassment of a student giving the wrong answer to a question. Most of us avoid this vulnerability and embarrassment, which is why most students raise their hands only when they feel certain of their answers.

Finally, there must be a trust in the dialogical process itself. We will subject ourselves to the work and vulnerability of dialogue only if we have some hope of its rewards. Dialogue requires trust in its process—to keep us at the work, to risk, to endure—all in the promise that something beneficial and true will emerge from the effort. We take the risk because of the promise of growth that can come only by way of dialogue. If, as is proposed in Chapter 7, the work of dialogue is consistent with the way of Jesus, then to trust the process of dialogue is much like following Jesus: we walk by faith, not by sight.

Growth in the Truth

Participants in healthy dialogue share a common desire to seek the truth that is beyond our human perspectives and self-interests. They come to the dialogue with their own convictions about truth, both intellectual and experiential. These understandings of truth will be offered and explored with care. At the same time, dialogue participants are aware that there is more truth than they can claim to know, that the truth of God, life, and eternity are beyond human knowing. Like Paul, they acknowledge that they "see through a darkened glass" (I Corinthians 13); but they do see, and they hold fast to what they see and bear witness to it.

Truth in this sense is more than an abstract, philosophical concept. It is also a pursuit of what is true in any given moral issue we may encounter: abortion, capital punishment, homosexuality, poverty. We come to these issues with strong convictions and rationales. We believe we know the truth; and yet, the truth is elusive, always beyond our grasp, larger than the capacity of our words.

Not everyone has a yearning to engage in a deeper pursuit of truth. The search for truth is too often replaced by a search for an advantage over an adversary. Perception and spin-doctoring become more important than the search for truth. Sometimes pursuing truth even means that our side doesn't get to convey the image of "winning."

Truth can disrupt the organization of our thoughts. It pushes us. It forces us to admit the limits of our knowing. This is uncomfortable, especially for church leaders, who often feel the pressure to appear confident and clear on all subjects. Preachers especially are encouraged to talk with certainty. Our medium is monologue, not dialogue. We know the answers; no other voices are needed. This attitude is the enemy of dialogue.

To seek truth we must develop an attitude of "cognitive modesty," to recognize that "[t]he message [of the Bible] points beyond our ability to apprehend perfectly[;] it points to that which is not yet part of historically available experience[;] it points to the coming kingdom of God. In this light, modesty and provisionality are not the result of weak-kneed accommodationism but are required by fidelity to the claims of the gospel" (Neuhaus, 1984, pp. 122–123).

In dialogue we open ourselves up to God, to a wisdom from Above that transcends the dialogue and sheds new light on our corporate discord and darkness. To enter into dialogue is to accept the possibility that God could choose to reveal truth through our adversary, or through a new self-discovery as we reveal ourselves before the other, or through the interchange of convictions.

A Place to Argue

If dialogue's insistence on humility and vulnerability sounds like a passive, apologetic exercise in civility—too polite to engage the important issues that divide us—then its role is still unclear. In fact, dialogue depends on a kind of controlled argument in order to help analyze and clarify the issue at hand. Plato called this dimension of dialogue "refutation." Through argument, passion enters the conversation and is the catalyst for the consistency and elaboration by both sides that can be the spark that ignites a new source of energy and light.

In dialogue, the question about argument is not "if" but "when." Arguments do not begin the dialogue, nor do they make up the bulk of the exchange. Words play a part without taking over the conversation. Arguments serve to deepen the bond between participants, not to polarize and terminate the conversation. David Tracy suggests that "[a]rguments function best when they are part of a whole. . . . Conversation should be the encompassing reality within which all good arguments find their being. Arguments belong within conversations and not visa versa" (1987, p. 24).

There is the danger that our arguments will become more important, more firm and unambiguous, than the truth we have experienced that gave birth to the convictions we argue about. This danger is very real for clergy, who are accustomed to using many words, carefully crafted, to express their thoughts. The words become excessive and take over. As Reuel Howe warns, "We are drenched by a monsoon of verbiage [that] dampens rather than illumines meaning" (1972, p. 6). This shower of words is a product of fear. It impairs our ability to use argument as a tool in the pursuit of truth. In dialogue, participants remember that the truth they seek to articulate is always truth that is both revealed to and concealed from us. Thus, good arguments within dialogue are balanced between conviction and humility.

A Definition of Dialogue

With these dimensions of dialogue in mind, we are prepared to consider a working definition of dialogue. The definition should be capable of succinctly describing the process in such a way that will attract potential participants. It should also govern the proceedings so that the intended results are achieved.

In his 1963 book, *The Miracle of Dialogue*, Reuel Howe defines dialogue as "that address and response between persons in which there is a flow of meaning between them in spite of all the obstacles that normally would block the relationship." It is to give oneself as one is to the other, and "to know the other as the other is" (p. 37). Later he adds, "It is communion in which we are mutually informed, purified, illumined, and reunited to ourselves, to one another, and God" (p. 106). The teamwork dimension of dialogue is evident in Howe's definition, as the "flow of meaning between" participants becomes a kind of mystical communion.

John Taylor, African missionary and Anglican Bishop, defines dialogue as "a sustained conversation between parties who are not saying the same thing and who recognize and respect the contradictions and mutual exclusions between their various ways of thinking" (quoted in Muck, 1995, p. 8). This definition presumes a tone of civility, a point or points of disagreement, and a commitment to talk over an extended period of time with the intention of actively exploring the nature and extent of the disagreement.

Leonard Swidler, a leader in interreligious dialogue, offers yet another definition: "Dialogue is a conversation on a common subject between two or more persons with differing views, the primary purpose of which is for each participant to learn from the other so that he or she can change and grow" (1983). The phrase "change and grow" recognizes the educational nature of dialogue.

Diana Eck defines dialogue simply as "mutual witness" and adds that "[d]ialogue does not mean that we will agree, but only that we will understand more clearly and that we will begin to replace ignorance, stereotype, even prejudice, with relationship. It is the language of mutuality, not power" (1993, p. 19). "Mutual witness" places dialogue within the activity of faithful living and suggests that dialogue emanates from our common experiences of grace and revelation, especially when the dialogue is between Christians. It moves dialogue out of the realm of competition and victors to a context where people convey their deepest convictions.

Linda Teurfs, a business organizational consultant, says that dialogue "creates meaning between [participants] . . . around what is trying to happen in the present moment," which implies "finding the next level of understanding." She emphasizes the need for participants to move out of the ruts of their individual patterns of thinking and into collective thinking with another person or with a group in order to explore something new that could be discovered in the very act of dialogue. "Dialogue is about seeing our personal issues as part of the larger community in which we take part" (1994, pp. 4, 8).

For our purposes as people seeking to shed more light and less heat on the many issues that split Christians today, I offer the following definition of dialogue: *Dialogue is an ongoing conversation between Christians of differing convictions who recognize their human limitations and who believe that God can use our various moral and theological conflicts to teach and re-form the church for holy living.*

This definition combines several key points from the previous definitions: we are human and thus always in need of further light and truth; our conflicting views are not problems to be reconciled, but distinct vantage points to help us identify and explore the key issues of our day as Christians; and because God is involved in the process of dialogue, a miracle is truly possible through dialogue. Dialogue defined in this way moves away from the tendency to "win" or "fix" the conflict; it works to place the process and the results in God's keeping, in God's time, and in God's way.

We still have a role as participants in the process, of course. If we remain silent, God will not work the dialogue miracle. If any participants in our dialogue lack hope in God, then God's desire to enter into the process may be seriously thwarted. If we prefer the predictable discomfort of conflict over the unpredictable discomfort of dialogue, then God may not give us the gifts of surprise. In short, if we are not willing to lay down our lives, God may not raise us up to a new plane of thought and possibilities.

Dialogue is grounded in hope. If culture-war soldiers say, "It is impossible to reason with them," or "The chasm is too wide," then dialogue is simply a temporary break from our respective monologues. If "There is nothing else to say to them," or if "There is nothing I care to hear from them," then dialogue degenerates into ammunition gathering, or worse, breaks out into battle. On the other hand, if our hope is not in ourselves or our ingenious plan for dialogue, but in the God who scripture attests is always doing something new, dialogue becomes an occasion laden with hope.

Other Forms of Communication: What Dialogue Is NOT

It is easy to confuse dialogue with other forms of interaction that are popular today. These other types of interaction are related to dialogue—cousins in the communications family that share several family traits, including the presence of a conflict, opposing sides coming together, and the stating of positions.

Here the similarities end. To mistake dialogue for one of its cousins is to miss the distinctiveness of dialogue from its family members. This section compares dialogue to other communication forms often confused with it. These communication forms are listed from the most adversarial to the least adversarial.

Debate

Debate denotes two clearly defined polarities about which each combatant argues in order to gain victory over the other. It is a win-lose battle. Debaters gain advantage over their adversaries by denying the subtle differences and similarities between the competing opinions. They reduce the argument to dramatic, simplified positions that are clear to the listeners and easily contained in a media sound bite or a bumper sticker. (James Davison Hunter's 1991 and 1994 works show how the media are guilty of reducing issues to simple, concise positions and inflaming the rhetoric while reducing the exploration of subtleties.) Participants speak from a position of certainty, extolling the virtue and superiority of their position and denouncing the limitations and fallacies of their opponents' position. They lock into their assigned positions with utter assurance and speak with care to avoid being contradicted. Statements from this form of interaction can turn personal, as in the 1988 vice-presidential debates when Lloyd Benson retorted to Dan Quayle, "I knew Jack Kennedy. . . . You're no Jack Kennedy."

Unfortunately, debate is the most common form of interaction within the religious community when we deal with issues of disagreement: point and counterpoint, people speaking for or against a motion, dissemination of brochures containing inflammatory rhetoric. After the appointed debate, which is typically little more than monologues from each side, a vote is taken to determine the temporary winner—temporary because losing sides rarely accede or go away. Debates "create losers who feel wronged and threatened, and winners who must keep a wary eye out for the conquered ones" (Becker and others, 1995, p. 145). This has been borne out in most of the Protestant denominational gatherings of the last twenty years, perhaps longer.

As Table 2.1 indicates, debate is vastly different from dialogue. Unlike debate, dialogue explores the complexities of issues rather than simplifying them. Facts and points of conviction are examined, questioned, placed in their larger context, and compared and contrasted with other convictions in order to check for consistency and clarity. Dialogue acknowledges that the church's beliefs constitute a "spectrum" (Woodbridge, 1995, p. 22) rather than a black-white, win-lose dichotomy of the issues. Dialogue avoids polarizing the church's positions into two choices, with the implication that one side is all good and the other side entirely bad, as, for example, conservative columnist Cal Thomas did when he stated, "We are asking people to follow one or the other way of thinking. . . . "

Dialogue is not based on winners and losers. To the contrary, it works to transcend the idea of opposing sides. It calls for a rather unnatural engagement—for adversaries to join together in the work of interpreting, listening, and recasting the issues for each other.

Table 2.1. Distinguishing Debate from Dialogue*

Debate	Dialogue
Pre-meeting communication between sponsors and participants is minimal and largely irrelevant to what follows.	Pre-meeting contacts and preparation of participants are essential elements of the full process.
Participants tend to be leaders known for propounding a carefully crafted position. The personas displayed in the debate are usually already familiar to the public. The behavior of the participants tends to conform to stereotypes.	Those chosen to participate are not necessarily outspoken "leaders." Whoever they are, they speak as individuals whose own unique experiences differ in some respect from others on their "side." Their behavior is likely to vary in some degree and along some dimensions from stereotypic images others may hold of them.
The atmosphere is threatening; attacks and interruptions are expected by participants and are usualy permitted by moderators.	The atmosphere is one of safety; facilitators propose, get agreement on, and enforce clear ground rules to enhance safety and promote respectful exchange.

Table 2.1. (continued)

Debate	Dialogue
Participants speak as representatives of groups.	Participants speak as individuals, from their own unique experience.
Participants speak to their own constituents and, perhaps, to the undecided middle.	Participants speak to each other.
Differences within "sides" are denied or minimized.	Differences among participants on the same "side" are revealed, as individual and personal foundations of beliefs and values are explored.
Partcipants express unswerving commitment to a point of view, approach, or idea.	Participants express uncertainties, as well as deeply held beliefs.
Participants listen in order to refute the other side's data and to expose faulty logic in their arguments. Questions are asked from a position	Participants listen to understand and gain insight into the beliefs and concerns of the others. Questions are asked from a position of curiosity.
Statements are predictable and offer little new information.	New information surfaces.
Success requires simple impassioned statements.	Success requires exploration of the complexities of the issue being discussed.
Debates operate within the constraints of the dominant public discourse. (The discourse defines the problem and the options for resolution. It assumes that fundamental needs and values are already clearly understood.)	Participants are encouraged to question the dominant public discourse, that is, to express fundamental needs that may or may not be reflected in the discourse and to explore various options for problem definition and resolution. Participants may discover inadequacies in the usual language and concepts used in the public debate.

* This table contrasts debate as commonly seen on television with the kind of dialogue we aim to promote in dialogue sessions conducted by the Public Conversations Project.

© 1992 Public Conversations Projects. Watertown, Mass.

Mediation

Mediation is a negotiating model that uses a neutral third party, a mediator, to attempt to resolve conflicts where a resolution or settlement is needed for a specific problem. It can substitute for parties turning to the legal system to decide the outcome of the dispute, for example, in divorces, employer-employee disputes, conflicts among family and friends, neighborhood disputes, or disagreements between consumers and merchants.

A neutral third party hears the facts from both parties and helps identify the key issue in the problem and locate common interests. A range of options are generated and discussed. The sides hone in on one option and fine-tune it with *bargaining* and *negotiation*. An effort is made to maximize everyone's interest by searching for a win-win solution. Finally, the decision is given a "reality test" and put into writing.

Conflicts over values and beliefs, such as the conflict between the religious Left and Right, are not dealt with in mediation because questions of values and beliefs are non-negotiable and thus cannot be mediated. However, the mediation model can reveal points of commonality among disputed value positions and offer solutions amenable to everyone. The skills and resources available from the fast-growing field of mediation are an excellent source of support for the work of dialogue between conflicting values and beliefs.

Mediation takes several different forms. *Facilitation* is a form of mediation for larger groups where help is needed to identify all the varied interests and to determine which elements should be considered in the decision-making process. A neutral third party helps the sides in dispute engage in discussion and enables the sides to work toward resolution.

Conflict resolution and *dispute resolution* are synonymous with mediation. These terms sometimes refer to a method for resolving day-to-day disputes within the workplace before issues reach the point of requiring formalized mediation. *Arbitration* is a formalized method of mediation wherein a third party is given authority, either by agreement of the sides or by a court of law, to act as a judge and to make a decision for parties who cannot agree.

Mediation in all its forms differs from dialogue because it is entered into as a way to move through a specific disagreement to a point of resolution. There is give and take, a kind of compromise. Usually the process depends on an outside mediator. Unlike mediation, the purpose of dialogue is not consensus or agreement, but conversation that may or may not bring the parties closer together. It is an "endless conversation" (McKenny, 1991, p. 428) in that it is an ongoing interchange, less focused on "getting to yes" (the title of Fisher and Ury's popular book on negotiation) than on knowing and being known. In dialogue, rather than seeing conflict as a problem to be resolved, the conflict becomes a teaching tool to be shared by all sides of the issue. It recognizes that "contrast is fundamental to understanding, for no subject, idea, or text is an island" (Graff, 1992, p. 108). Dialogue does not try to move toward a solution but to create an atmosphere where understanding and growth happen.

Compromise

Compromise is an agreement reached between opposing parties wherein each party makes significant concessions in its original positions in order to meet the opposition at some approximate half-way point. It is striking a bargain. Ideally, the concessions made on each side are equal in sacrifice. It may be that neither side is entirely happy with the agreement, but each is willing to accept it in order to move beyond an impasse and reach a decision.

Because compromise is such a prevalent technique in our bargaining culture, it is often presumed that accepting compromise is a necessary element in dialogue. This becomes a major impediment to parties on the Left and Right who are invited to dialogue, for neither side is willing to compromise its convictions. If dialogue is simply a set-up for compromise, then indeed in many cases "we have nothing to talk about," for deeply held convictions cannot be bargained away. In matters of faith, compromise is a form of unfaithfulness.

If, on the other hand, dialogue's task is to present our real and substantive differences in a forum of honest interchange, then there is a great deal to talk about. Dialogue's task is listening and clarifying, not compromising and striking a bargain. It is not about changing, except perhaps as a by-product of discoveries made in the course of the conversation, which is always a gift.

Collaboration

Collaboration, consensus-building, and *group facilitation* bring together conflicted parties in order to address a specific issue that may be unrelated to the issue of conflict but is a shared concern that cannot be resolved separately; for example, the religious and medical communities collaborate when they come together to address public health issues.

Collaboration has built-in limitations but also is a necessary form of interaction. As one leader who brings diverse groups together acknowledges, "Collaboration assumes that different groups need not blend or unify. It is not built on the naive idea that collaborators could ever expect to find a common vocabulary, or single faith. It does not assume that we will naturally drift together; it assumes the opposite, knowing from painful history that it is more natural to distrust and fear, more natural to drift apart into ever defensive circles of us and ours" (Gunderson, n.d., p. 17).

Collaboration is more goal-oriented than dialogue. It politely "agrees to disagree," to set aside differences temporarily in order to complete a given task. There are times when collaboration is the appropriate course of action, but this is a significantly different enterprise from dialogue, where disagreements are not masked or set aside, but put in the center of the table as the subject of discussion. Collaboration can proceed from dialogue, as has been the case in dialogues around abortion; and conversely, collaboration may be the impetus to begin dialogue, as has been the case with people joined together to address violence among children. Nevertheless, these remain different forms of communication.

Discussion

In *discussion*, different views are presented and defended but with little sense of a purpose for the interaction. Ideas are knocked around, hit back and forth like a Ping-Pong ball. (The word "discussion" comes from the same root as "percussion" and "concussion"; this root means hitting, breaking apart, or fragmenting.) Healthy discussion has an open, nonthreatening flow in that issues of power and winning are not present. Similarly, in *fact-finding* or *comparison*, differences and similarities are noted in order to clarify the nature of the disagreement for future confrontations. One party says, "I think this." "Well good," says the other party; "I think something else." Freedom and trust to express oneself exist in discussion, but unlike dialogue, little substantive merging or exploration of the differences takes place. And although discussion is open-ended like dialogue, it lacks dialogue's focused purpose of seeking growth and discovery by the participants.

Group Therapy

Finally, *group therapy* is a conversation among people who share feelings and insights for other participants to hear and respond to. The purpose of the gatherings is to facilitate the personal growth of each member of the group. In hearing the views and experiences of others, participants receive personal insight and growth. When participants share their views before others and receive feedback, they experience additional insight and growth. Although dialogue also celebrates insight and growth, the intent of dialogue is not personal growth, but collective growth. Dialogue emphasizes shared meaning that emerges from our individual positions.

Other Religious Dialogues

The long and important histories of dialogue in the church should inform our current attempts at culture war dialogue. *Ecumenical dialogue* has occurred over the last half century among various groups within the Christian community around particular doctrinal questions and the faith and practice they engender. This ongoing dialogue has produced understanding and a sense of mutuality. Similarly, *interreligious dialogue* is the ongoing conversation among representatives of the great religions of the world, who increasingly live side by side in our cultures. The purpose of these dialogues is to nurture understanding and mutual respect. For the Christian community, these dialogues have also yielded both deeper understanding of our neighbors' faith as well as awareness of the depth and power of our own faith traditions.

The most notable ecumenical and interreligious dialogues happen in formal settings with appointed representatives. These dialogues are also happening in unofficial ways every day among ordinary people in our pluralistic culture. Both forms of dialogue are important. Grace and healing have been the result in many cases.

These dialogues have also taught us a great deal about the nature and limits of dialogue. They have uncovered effective techniques for dialogue: civility, patience, the use of language, and the conviction that truth is more than simply the least common denominator or the sum of the parts of dialogue (Muck 1995). These resources are valuable for our fledgling work of culture war dialogue.

At the same time, dialogue in our current Christian culture wars is a different kind of encounter from ecumenical and interreligious dialogues. Dialogue over polarizing issues within the Christian church often centers on moral questions, with the sides less clearly defined than in ecumenical or interreligious dialogues. An additional distinction is that the conflicts dividing the Christian church today pit us against fellow or former church members, classmates, and family members. We work together in community ministries or within the same denominational structures. We have a more immediate shared history. These relationships make the issues for dialogue more impassioned and divisive, for there is simply more at stake for us emotionally and institutionally. Christian culture war dialogue is far more than an intellectual exercise or benign exploration of uncharted territories. It begins with a struggle over something basic and dear: How will we—church and society—order our life together? Do we see our culture war adversary as The Enemy against whom we are called into battle by our faith? Or is someone or something else our true common enemy?

One other distinction of this newer dialogue is that we have no national body to call us together, whereas ecumenical and interreligious dialogue is often initiated by the National and World Councils of Churches or the National Conference of Christians and Jews. The transdenominational, multilevel conflict that faces the Christian church in the United States today has no structure, no formal context for the dialogue to take place. No mutually accepted leaders are present to preside, set the ground rules, and keep us on track.

The result is that there are no popular models of dialogue. This void leaves us asking, "What would dialogue look like?" The following chapters will suggest some models that help fill this void.

The Limits of Dialogue

Before exploring the many important contributions that dialogue can make to the church's current conflicts, it bears saying that occasionally dialogue is not the answer to a conflict. Having built a case for dialogue as an invaluable resource for conflicts within the church, I must also point out the limitations of dialogue. I hesitate to do so because of the danger that people will use dialogue's limitations as an escape hatch whenever the work becomes too demanding or too threatening. Nevertheless, we must acknowledge that sometimes dialogue is *not* the appropriate action for people of faith. There are times to talk, and times to be silent. Following are some instances when dialogue is not the proper strategy.

- Obviously, we cannot dialogue if either side refuses to talk or listen. To continue to pursue dialogue in the face of absolute rejection by the other side may be counterproductive. In my experience, this refusal to dialogue comes more often from the Right than from the Left, because the Right's beliefs easily lead to an "absolute absolutism," which construes dialogue as weakness or as an action that might inadvertently legitimate the opposition's beliefs. Thus, the conflict strategy of some on the Right becomes, "Take no prisoners"; that is, they work to completely overtake the opposition until they are gone. This attitude can be found among those on the extreme Left as well, although they are not as vocal or as public about their sentiments. (A more helpful strategy might be to engage in dialogue with those on the other side who are willing to be in dialogue and to ask them in turn to convey your positions to those on the extreme edges of their side. People on both extremes may be able to dialogue only with others who are closer to the middle of the spectrum, but still on their side, instead of dialoguing with people from the other side.)

On some occasions, those who attempt to engage in dialogue should heed the instruction of Jesus to "shake the dust off our feet" as a testimony against those who will not listen or speak (Matthew 10:14). When the adversary refuses to listen or speak, it may be time to move on. As Bruce Ackerman concluded, "I can use neither force nor reason to impose dialogue on you. All I can do is ask my question and await your reply. If you try to stare me down and impose brute force upon me, I will act in self-defense. If, instead, you answer my questions, I will answer yours, and we will see what we will see. The choice is yours" (1980, p. 374).

It is essential, however, to remember that Jesus continues to pursue those who are estranged (Luke 15:3–7) and keeps knocking at the closed door (Revelation

3:20) in hopes of restoring a relationship with a brother or sister. Doors are not walls. It is not the nature of doors to stay closed forever, and Christians committed to dialogue hold on to this hope. We consider the causes for the closed door, look for constructive changes to the dialogue format, and continue to knock.

- Dialogue must also be abandoned when it is co-opted by persons in power. This happens when dialogue is used by an oppressive group as a way to appease a group with a grievance. In this case, dialogue is no longer a genuine exchange, but simply a way to neutralize the cries of those without power. In this situation, dialogue is converted from a tool for mutual understanding and transformation to a salve that soothes the feelings of the aggrieved by giving them the illusion of being heard and taken seriously. This perversion of dialogue will eventually be exposed, as the offended party comes to recognize that, indeed, this "talk is cheap." This pseudo dialogue should be halted immediately and postponed until both sides agree to engage in genuine dialogue in good faith.

- Dialogue should also be halted when it is being substituted for the work of counseling. Disputes can be the result of something more complex than a misunderstanding or even competing world views. Sometimes the sides involved in a dispute are hampered by serious dysfunction. The two sides are so entrenched in destructive patterns of communication that it would be impossible to enter into substantive, constructive dialogue. When this is the case, dialogue only serves to intensify the symptoms of the dysfunction and cause greater division. Dialogue should be postponed until counseling begins and there is some measure of growth. At that point, dialogue may serve to enhance the counseling process.

One word of warning: Participants in heated dialogue are often quick to accuse their adversaries of being "crazy," thus justifying their decision to walk away from the dialogue. The determination that the dialogue ought to be postponed should be made only by someone well qualified, and only if absolutely necessary.

- The most important and complex reason for halting dialogue is when it is being misused to protect an unjust action. Dialogue is a tool for correcting misunderstandings and for deepening our understanding of those with whom we disagree. It is *not* the goal or highest virtue of the Christian life. Some conflicts are more than a difference of perspectives. As Martin Luther King, Jr., reminded us in "Letters from a Birmingham Jail," sometimes there are reasons "why we can't wait." Christians cannot be content to engage in dialogue with perpetrators of evil and injustice. We must be hesitant and cautious to place such strong labels on an individual or group, but sometimes we must.

There are times when the light of dialogue must give way to the purifying, prophetic fire of the Spirit, when action must take precedent over talk, when conflict must be pursued in place of a false peace. Jeremiah recommended such action when he accused the prophets of Jerusalem: "They have treated the wound of my people carelessly, saying, 'Peace, peace,' when there is no peace" (6:14). A dialogue between Rosa Parks and the Montgomery bus company that tried to force her to give up her seat in the 1950s was not the appropriate action at that time. Clearly, the time for talking had passed. An act of resistance, a shifting of sentiment, and a redefinition of power was necessary before honest dialogue could resume.

From Division to Dialogue

If dialogue is heated because it is being misused to harbor injustice, then honest, clear dialogue should resume once the act of prophetic resistance is complete. As Christians, we are not able to terminate permanently our interaction with our enemies. Stands of opposition and resistance, when they achieve their goals, are always followed by a season of dialogue. It is the way of Christ.

Dialogue is difficult. It is far easier, and a more natural reaction, to simmer from the heat of battle than to transform the conflict into a light that is able to spotlight our strengths and expose our weaknesses. In order to entice Christians in conflict to move from their division to dialogue, we need to show them some of the benefits of entering this risky, sometimes uncomfortable work. What is the prize of dialogue? What are the benefits? Is it really possible that by interacting with our enemies we can actually become more fully the people that God is calling us to be? Chapter Three explores some of the benefits that await those who will take dialogue's step of faith.

3

Naming Our Fears

Dialogue is effortful. Thorough, frank exchanges of views take place occasionally between two people of opposing conviction who find themselves in the right place at the right time and in the right frame of mind to speak and listen with care and courage. This, however, is an exception rather than the norm. Dialogue usually requires some intentionality. And if, as I have suggested, formal dialogue is virtually nonexistent, then little dialogue is taking place around the country on the church's many topics of conflict.

This absence of dialogue must end. Grassroots dialogue is essential in order for the church—global and local—to minimize its infighting and regain its corporate voice and strength. If the church is to break out of its self-destructive divisions and rediscover its role as peacemaker and transformer, then in every community across the country someone must start a dialogue—an ongoing conversation among Christians of differing convictions who recognize their limitations and who believe that God can use our various moral and theological conflicts to teach and reform the church for holy living.

But who will begin the dialogue? What kind of pastors and lay leaders would give themselves to the work of dialogue? Like the story of "The Little Red Hen," most pastors and laity favor the *idea* of dialogue and would be glad to benefit from its results. But "Who will help me plant the seed, pick the grain, grind the meal . . . ?"

With varied demands competing for our time and attention, how can we hope to entice the right people to respond to the call to this difficult and sometimes thankless work? How do we begin to bring together people from diverse Christian perspectives? And what would dialogue look like in the midst of our polarized culture today?

Getting Started

Beginning the dialogue is the most critical and perhaps the trickiest part of the endeavor. A wide array of factors blend to dissuade potential participants from entering into dialogue. Instead, these factors promote the game-playing mode people are already familiar with. To make dialogue possible, two key obstacles must be overcome: fear and futility.

Beyond Fear

All of us have fears. Dialogue, because of the nature of the endeavor, can expose and even exacerbate these fears in revealing ways. Our fear can come from one or more sources: the fear of being in the presence of one's "enemy"; fear that one will lose face through a misstatement or an inconsistency; fear of losing one's position; fear of violence (physical or verbal) if dialogue turns into an ambush; fear of losing control; or fear of widening the gap between us and our adversaries. Whatever the source, the presence of fear typically shuts down the possibility of creative and constructive communication. (For an excellent treatment on the effects of fear in communication processes, see Speed Leas' *Leadership and Conflict*, 1982.)

For example, a Sunday school class was wrestling repeatedly with the question of universalism: Does God's grace include all people eventually, or does God permit some people's actions to condemn them to hell? The class, comprised of long-time church members and close friends, was split on the issue. Through the loving, inviting leadership of the class teacher, healthy and invigorating dialogue emerged from time to time. Unfortunately, one of the brightest and most passionate members of the group found these kinds of exchanges extremely threatening. On the one hand, his deep convictions about a God of justice made him want to weigh in on the issue and advocate for his position. It also compelled him to try to better understand the thinking of those who differed from him. On the other hand, he had a deep fear that to speak his mind would result in his losing the friendships he valued within the class. Prior experiences in conversations of disagreement programmed him to expect that if he took an unpopular position it could cause others to reject him. His fear paralyzed his ability to dialogue and thus diminished the class discussion.

To enable people to engage in dialogue we must take their fears seriously and help them alleviate or at least assuage them. One way is by helping people name their fears, perhaps beginning with the dialogue initiator naming and honestly owning the fears that he or she feels. The one initiating the dialogue may "admit" to the potential dialogue participant, "There are lots of reasons that I am personally hesitant to explore a dialogue with people on the other side," and then begin to enumerate them. "Can you think of other reasons people might be hesitant?" he or she can ask. It is preferable to avoid asking, "What are *you* afraid of?" When we are afraid, claiming our own fears may be the last thing we want to do; however, we might include them in a list of what *others* might fear. As the fears are named, the initiator can begin to explain in a calm, assuring manner that dialogue's process and ground-rules ensure a healthy experience to be welcomed rather than feared.

Fears are reduced when participants know what they are getting into and are convinced that both the stated and actual agendas are not to defeat, humiliate, or threaten them in any way. People considering dialogue must know that they are entering an atmosphere of neutrality and respect for all involved. One way to meet this need is by agreeing to a set of guidelines that will govern the dialogue.

Potential participants in a Christian dialogue may want to consider the following Ten Guidelines for Dialogue:

1. *Risk*. We will face our differences. We will consider all views and information, even if they conflict with our basic assumptions about the issue and result in conclusions that differ from our own.

2. *Respect*. We will cultivate respect for our dialogue partners as human beings and as fellow Christians. We will take each other's views and convictions seriously. We will not question one another at the point of sincerity or Christian commitment.

3. *Fairness*. We will not judge people on the other side by popular stereotypes or by their least admirable expressions. We will allow people to define themselves, rather than presuming to know them from inference, categorization, or outside observation. We will allow those on the other side the freedom to restate, change, or expand their position in the course of the dialogue without interpreting these actions as a sign of weakness, confusion, or ambivalence.

4. *Humility*. We acknowledge that our understanding of God and the things of God is limited and finite. We recognize that issues requiring dialogue are often complex and ambiguous, even when they appear straightforward from one particular vantage point, and that no one has a final answer to the question at hand. We will avoid the presumption of oversimplification.

5. *Teamwork*. We will work together as partners with those on the other side of the issue in order to learn something new about our own position, their position, or a new position yet to be discovered.

6. *Openness*. We will be open about the nature of our disagreement and will test our assumptions about where the points of

disagreement are. We will not judge the correctness or ortho-
doxy of a position solely by how it relates to our own position.

7. *Listening*. We will stand next to people on the other side and
attempt to hear the issue from their place. We will avoid for-
mulating our response while another is speaking. We will
attempt to empathize with the other side's point of view.

8. *First-Person Speech*. We will limit our speaking to the information, materials, and evidence we have available to us. We will
focus on how we can deepen our understanding of the other
side and narrow the gap from our side, rather than worry or
complain about what the other side will or will not do.

9. *Depth*. We will explore the complexity of needs, interests,
feelings, and convictions that underlie the various positions
on the issue. We will search for the secondary, interconnected
issues and assumptions behind the presenting issue. We will
be cautious of quick, easy solutions that appear to heal
instantly or convert others to our side, but merely mask the
point of disagreement.

10. *Patience*. Because we recognize that good dialogue is always a
sustained conversation, we will stay with the process and not
avoid or abandon the dialogue.

In formal dialogues, participants may need to explore or amend
these Ten Guidelines (as in Chapter Four) through one or more pre-
dialogue meetings, much like national representatives do before
their heads of state engage in talks. The Common Ground Network
for Life and Choice, a national group that facilitates dialogues,
assists communities in the logistics of bringing together groups in
conflict. They begin by creating a steering committee comprised of
representatives from both sides. The committee then meets to
explore the common-ground concept, to develop a sense of common purpose and trust, and to plan a jointly sponsored dialogue
workshop.

The steering committee agrees on ground rules that ensure safety and respect, based on what the committee believes participants need to be assured that they will feel comfortable in the conversation. A lead facilitator, someone from the Common Ground Network staff, trains volunteers to be small-group facilitators. Usually the volunteers are people who already have skills in this type of work, such as counselors, mediators, and teachers. The dialogue itself includes people from the community who represent the range of convictions on the issue at hand, with generally equal numbers representing the various sides of the issue in question. The Common Ground Network has found that informing candidates for dialogue of these checks and balances helps to quell fears and pique the interest of people who care passionately about a topic. (See the appendix, "Additional Resources for Dialogue," for information on Common Ground Network for Life and Choice.)

In less formal, more spontaneous dialogue settings, such as family conversations or Sunday school classes, the creation of a "safe place" for a frank and thorough exchange of views is more subjective, based on the attitude projected by the dialogue initiator and the feelings perceived by those invited into dialogue. The guidelines are not explicitly listed and reviewed; no moderator is assigned; participants have no awareness that "we are engaged in dialogue." Rather, in the course of a conversation, a controversy surfaces by one or more groups or individuals, and it is possible that, rather than a debate or a discussion, a dialogue is born.

Opening sentences set the mood for the exchange. Do people feel challenged to defend a position or invited to offer their views? Unfortunately, the same opening statement can be perceived either as a challenge or an invitation. For example, "I'd like to know why you think women can be ordained as pastors" can cause defensive walls to rise, or the very same statement can be heard as a genuine request for explanation and insight.

Slowing the pace of the interchange is another way to alleviate fears, both in formal and informal dialogues. This may require backing off a few notches from the level of intensity that we feel and allowing the person with whom we disagree to get comfortable with the process of talking about a divisive issue. It is possible, with tone of voice, body language, and physical proximity to an adversary, to create a more relaxed and inviting context in which to deal with the issue.

What is said, when it is said, and how it is said (and heard) all impact the level of fear a person feels when considering whether to engage in dialogue. Remaining aware of the many fears people bring to a conversation about a divisive issue, and carefully framing the issue and inviting participation in a dialogue, will go a long way toward bringing people into the exchange in a healthy, open way.

Beyond Futility

Another key obstacle to dialogue is the assumption that constructive conversation with those with whom we deeply disagree is an exercise in futility. As one leader from the Left complained when invited into a dialogue, "There is a fundamentalist mentality that is impervious to discussion. They put a negative spin on everything you say."

This attitude was repeatedly expressed in interviews with several pastors from across the theological spectrum who were recently asked to consider using dialogue as a possible tool for healing the church's divisions. A pastor on the Right contended, "The other side is engaged in an ongoing sinful state. This makes dialogue impossible for a person of faith." A Left pastor, when asked about the conflicts between the religious Left and Right, concluded, "We are absolutely at cross-purposes. It is hard to hold a common ground together when one wants to use the ground as a garden while the other wants to use it for a toxic waste dump." From the Right, another pastor held firm: "More important than dialogue is the quest for truth. I don't think we should emphasize unity at the cost of truth." Another Left pastor declared that it is impossible to dialogue when the other side's views are coming solely from an emotional, irrational prejudice: "You can't reason people out of a position that they didn't reason themselves into. You can't build a bridge between prejudice and anything else."

The sense of futility expressed in these attitudes toward dialogue can be gently, but firmly, countered from several fronts. Begin by acknowledging to the speaker that the view expressed has some basis in fact. (This acknowledgment lets the person know that you take him or her seriously and value his or her perspective.) Then offer some gently-worded alternatives to the feeling of futility:

- Remember that the speaker's view is neither the only word nor the final word on the subject.

- It is dangerous to overgeneralize, for example, to assume that everyone on the other side thinks and acts the same way that people encountered in the past have thought and acted.

- Consider the mystery of the future: the past does not determine the future, especially within the framework of people of faith. God is at work, always and every- where seeking to do a new thing.

In dialogue, God is able to break through a sense of futility by allow- ing our differences to bring clarity to the deepest concerns and fears we bring to the conflict. Conflicts occur because we care about the outcome of certain community decisions. As these conflicts develop, we are not always clear at the outset about the real nature of our concerns. Dialogue helps us distinguish between our *real* concerns and our *stated* concerns. In the give-and-take of dialogue, our con- cerns are defined and refined, not compromised. This give-and-take produces a better understanding of the problem and a wider range of solutions than we would have achieved on our own.

. . . .

Consider, for example, the story of a congregation polarized over whether the U.S. flag should remain in its sanctuary. One side insisted that the flag be removed. The other side insisted that the flag remain. In the course of the dialogue, each side's underlying concerns were gradually uncovered. The first group's concern was that the presence of the flag gave the wrong impression to those who entered the sanctuary; namely, that the church's allegiance was to the state instead of to Christ. Further, they believed the church should present itself as an international body, rather than allied to one nation alone. The second group's concern was that our country and the freedom it had brought us through the sacrifice of others should be respected and remembered by the presence of the flag. Good Christians, they believed, should be loyal and grateful citizens.

The initial concerns were incompatible and irresolvable; the flag could not both remain and be removed from the sanctuary. But as the sides began to explore their underlying concerns, they discovered that their real concerns, while still different, were not incompatible: one group wanted it clear that the church's allegiance was to Christ and that the church was for all people; the second group wanted to show gratitude for religious freedom and respect for the state. From these clarified positions, new options were generated: placing the flag in the foyer of the church; having special worship services that express gratitude for religious freedom; or placing flags of all U.N. countries in the sanctuary. These new options were discovered through the refinement of concerns and convictions that resulted from the process of dialogue (Stutzman and Schrock-Shenk, 1995, p. 163).

• • • • • • •

Issues such as those revealed through dialogue on the sanctuary flag conflict are called *convergent issues*. Dialogue helps to bring adversaries together to a previously unknown position where everyone's views converge. Dialogue on convergent issues can be exciting, like solving a riddle or cracking a mystery novel.

Unfortunately, some issues are not resolvable in such a neat, conciliatory fashion. These are called *divergent issues* because the more the underlying concerns of the two sides are revealed through dialogue, the more the two sides diverge, or move away from each other. When we dialogue on divergent issues, we must be satisfied with a different kind of reward: participants having a deeper understanding of the issues, yet remaining open to new ways of relating to those whose convictions differ from their own.

Another key source of futility is a lack of clarity about exactly whom or what we are up against in our conflicts. As dialogue reveals our underlying concerns, it also begins to clarify the identities of our real adversaries. In many cases, Christians will discover that their enemy is not another Christian group, as is often assumed. We may have substantial disagreements with other Christians that make us adversaries on one level; but to identify each other as the real foe may have us fighting the wrong battles, as cartoon characters who are friends wrestle and fight each other while the opponent stands safely to the side.

Who is "the enemy"? People of faith have given countless answers to this question. Through dialogue the church continues to wrestle with diverse views about the enemy's identity and location. Dialogue prods the church to seek out the greater, genuine enemy and to refine the best methods for doing battle in the name of the Lord.

In the course of dialogue with our front-line adversaries, we also gain the practical benefit of greater clarity about ourselves and our distinctions from others. Adversaries help define us. In the early church, when Marcion listed gospels and epistles that he considered authoritative for the church, leaving out several key writings, the Church was forced to decide what it did and did not consider canonical. This conflict became an occasion for clarity for the young church. Dialogue can provide similar clarity for the church today as we listen to the views of our adversaries and as we hear the echo of our views through their interpretive filters.

Dialogue: Soul Exercise

Beyond addressing fear and futility as dialogue's dual impediments, the most compelling motivation for bringing hesitant participants to the dialogue table is the unique opportunity for personal growth that dialogue offers. Dialogue can be a kind of gymnasium for the soul, working over an extended period of time to stretch and grow participants spiritually, relationally, intellectually, and emotionally. It is an opportunity to determine one's emotional strengths and weaknesses. It turns Christian platitudes such as "love your enemy" and "go the second mile" into real-life activities, and it brings us face-to-face with people we avoid or miss in our daily routines.

Spiritual Growth

Despite the modern tone that the term "dialogue" connotes, dialogue is in fact a very old scriptural endeavor (as shown in Chapter Seven). Dialogue is one of the key ways that we humans act out what it means to live faithfully as children of God. Few other endeavors are so directly modeled after the way of God or call for such a high level of dependence on God. Substantial dialogue calls for prayerful personal preparation. It anticipates the tangible working of God in and through the chaos of human conflict. To dialogue is to embody the practices of grace, humility, forgiveness, trust, and love.

* * * * * * *

For example, Susan described a major conflict she had a year earlier with Joy, a member of her church, over whether a candidate who had been recommended by a search committee was the right person for a staff position in their church. Susan had voted against the candidate; Joy had voted for her. When the votes were counted and the candidate was narrowly rejected, the church was deeply pained, and the women's relationship was strained to near-breaking point. "I knew we couldn't simply call a truce or wait for the pain to heal," remembered Susan. "We needed to talk together about our convictions and talk through our differences. Finally, about a year later, during one of the free periods in a women's retreat, I approached Joy and named the chasm between us. It was one of the hardest things I've ever done, but she agreed to talk through the issues that separated us.

"There was something mystical about our conversation: Neither of us got mad or defensive, which would have been easy to do. We began by talking about our common love for our church. Eventually, I asked her to tell me one more time why she thought the candidate was the right person for our church, and I really tried to listen carefully and intently. For the first time I was able to see things from her perspective and to find some qualities in the candidate that I hadn't seen before. It made me feel a lot different about her and her vote. The qualities I saw wouldn't have been enough to have changed my position, but I was able to say to her, 'You know, if I had been able to see [the candidate] in the way you did, I would have been more likely to vote for her too.' Joy seemed glad to hear me acknowledge this.

"Then Joy asked me what I had seen and why I had voted against [the candidate]. I think she learned some things she hadn't considered before, probably not enough to convince her that I was right, but enough to see my point of view and to appreciate the fact that I wasn't simply trying to be divisive or stubborn.

"It's odd," said Susan. "In a way, nothing changed; we both had the same convictions we had before the conversation. But somehow, by the end of the process, a kind of divine healing had taken place. God was with us in a very real way. I think it happened because we were both vulnerable and willing to hear the other person out."

• • • • • • •

Dialogue opens us up to the work of God in new and unexpected places. It creates the kind of tiny opening that is enough for God's Spirit to slip in and do new things.

Relational Growth

The story of Susan and Joy shows that to listen carefully and receptively to another person creates a bond between the listener and the speaker. When we see someone earnestly seeking to understand our position, even if the person is not able to share our conviction, we feel valued and respected, and we reciprocate. In some cases, dialogue gives birth to relationship; in others, a relationship is already established, and it improves the dialogue, which in turn deepens the relationship.

The Paired Congregations model, a project of the Study Circles Resource Center (see Resource A), offers the possibility of a growing relationship between dialogue partners by linking two churches within a reasonable geographic distance whose members voluntarily agree to enter into a series of dialogues on an issue of mutual concern. These churches may come from different denominations, different racial or ethnic backgrounds, or different geographic areas of the community.

Participants in Paired Congregations agree to learn from different views and experiences and to review preselected printed materials (for example, newspaper or magazine articles) to supplement the discussions. Leaders secure reading materials and a discussion leader—someone willing to remain neutral and to withhold his or her own views—to guide the process.

Session 1 sets the ground rules for dialogue and explores the participants' connections with the issue, guided by the questions, "Why are you concerned about this issue?" and "How have your experiences or concerns influenced your opinions about this issue?"

Session 2 examines the variety of views about the issue being considered and asks, "What are the genuine concerns that underlie this view?" and "What experiences and beliefs might lead decent and caring people to support that point of view?" Also considered are the trade-offs inherent in each point of view.

Session 3 looks at the issue from a faith perspective. Participants take turns reading scripture and other sources and explaining how their faith impacts their position. Listeners hear firsthand an alternative view of the issue held by another person of faith. This process allows listeners to see the complexity of the issue and the tensions among competing key values within our faith.

Session 4 asks, "What can we do?" with the conflict and tension of our dissimilar views. The two groups leave open the possibility of joining together in an action that addresses a common concern discovered through the dialogue.

This model brings together several key elements for successful dialogue. The format enables the dialogue to be carried out over an extended period of time, thus giving the experience time to gel and grow. Another strength is that, unlike other community dialogue formats, this model involves people already joined together in their respective churches, which deepens their own sense of community within their church, while at the same time linking them with people in their city with whom they may not have had previous contact.

Sessions 2 and 3 enable people to speak from their deepest convictions and also to hear others with whom they disagree do the same. By postponing the scriptural focus of the disputed issue until Session 3, participants have an opportunity to build relationships and to get acquainted with the tone of the dialogue before employing the scriptures—often the point of breakdown in the church's many disputes. This delay in introducing scripture may appear to be a weakness in the model for people who want to begin the dialogue by examining the scripture; however, appealing to scripture tends to halt the dialogue before it begins.

Often dialogue is born out of relationships that are already in place, rather than being the catalyst for new relationships. For example, seminary student David Mauldin wrote an article describing the dynamics between students who had ongoing theological disagreements while living together in a single men's dormitory (1995). Many of the conflicts between theologically conservative and theologically progressive seminary students were predictable and typical. What was revealing was how dialogue was tempered and shaped by these students' co-existence as single males preparing for ministry and living in a communal setting on a seminary campus.

The students were frank and firm in conviction; at the same time they were sensitive and loving. They had the ability to separate the passion and discomfort of the conflict from the fact that their adversary was a housemate and a human being. Disputes could be harsh and personal, but were forgotten when they were over. As one student said, "We debate all the time (sometimes we agree); then the next day he is giving me directions to Lexington."

A common interest in women also helped the students transcend their differences. Mauldin noted, "You may know that this guy thinks you are the strangest theological aberration since David Koresh, but if a member of the opposite sex has treated him poorly, you rally to his side. The guy across the hall could not exegete a Dr. Seuss book, but has a date this weekend, and you are happy for him."

Within the church, the issues that divide us are important and must be discussed; however, as Mauldin notes, we must "put them in their place." These students discovered that, rising above the issues that divided them, was the fact of their common humanity. When this reality pressed itself on them, as in the case of a fellow student in deep financial need, "our differences did not matter any more."

In dialogue we learn to appreciate more deeply the role that other people play both in our personal growth, and more importantly, in the possibility of discovering the collective meaning among us, which is a deeper, more valuable understanding of an issue than any one of us can discern on our own. We need each other. Without another view in tension with our own, we are not forced to explore an issue more deeply. We begin to realize the value of an "adversary," not only in the dialogue process, but in virtually every area of life that calls for exploring issues beyond the scope of our limited sight. Thus, dialogue changes the way we interact with others in everyday life.

Intellectual Growth

Without dialogue, we can assume that the level of thinking and exploring that we've already completed is sufficient for the issue in question. Most people in our culture avoid the possibility of dialogue—perhaps in part because they anticipate the challenge of such an endeavor. Intellectual couch potatoes abound, resulting in soft thinkers.

Dialogue gets us off the couch and into the mental gym. It pulls us from the warm cocoon of familiar faces and voices and pushes us into a circle of people who, sometimes to our surprise, have conflicting but well-reasoned views different from ours. Within the church, for example, it is more comfortable and less quarrelsome to associate only with like-minded people. In some cases, this insulation from adversaries is not intentional but is simply the result of the limited circles in which we move. As a result, we may not be aware of the larger spectrum of positions within the broader church, because everyone we know agrees with us. As one person naively said at a denominational meeting, in shocked response to losing a vote on a controversial issue, "How could we have lost? Everyone I know voted the same way I did!"

Dialogue pushes participants to hone their deepest convictions and critique their underlying assumptions. The disciplines of dialogue—thinking, listening, articulating, and clarifying—refine our thinking and invite us to explore new dimensions of the issues in conflict.

Dialogue should not be used as a type of deposition wherein we gain access to the views and positions of those with whom we disagree, but it does serve to help us better understand our adversary. This knowledge can increase our ability to promote and defend the position we hold dear. As a participant in dialogues on abortion said, "it educates [us] on the real concerns that need to be addressed. . . .

Both sides are plagued with distorted impressions of what the other side believes."

A bold approach to dialogue comes from the education field. In *Beyond the Culture Wars*, Gerald Graff describes the battle in college English departments between proponents of traditional literature and modern literature, and he proposes that, rather than quelling the conflict with a polite civility, the department should intentionally and publicly "teach the conflicts themselves" (1992, p. 12). Let students be exposed to the conflicting views that incite war in the faculty lounge between the traditionalists and modernists.

Graff suggests that "in a country where literature has not exactly been high on the list of national priorities, there is something a bit bizarre about the belief that the eruption of a passionate quarrel over literature is bad for it. . . . The classics, I suggest, have less to fear from newfangled ideological hostility than from old-fashioned indifference. . . . The best way to kill the classics has always been to put them on a pedestal, safe from the contemporary forces that challenge them" (pp. 47, 50).

Conflict, when made public as an ongoing dialogue, could positively energize the issue by bringing passion and conviction to the surface. Rather than a private battle, let it be a dialogue. Taking advantage of the culture war within the English department will inspire a deeper appreciation for both the traditional *and* the modern forms of literature and will create a context where new light can break forth on everyone involved in the interchange.

A parallel exists between the university English departments' culture wars and the church's many areas of cultural and theological conflict. The so-called experts—professors and pastors—have too often fought their culture war battles in private—in the faculty lounge, the church parking lot, or the hallways of the denominational meeting—and away from the view of students and laypeople. These are typically poorly fought, quickly staged, and minimally substantive battles that fail to employ our best resources. The result is a constituency unable to understand or appreciate what is at stake in these skirmishes. It is a missed opportunity for education and inspiration.

The university and the church are both called to fulfill a "contradictory mission[:] . . . to preserve, transmit, and honor our traditions, yet at the same time . . . to produce new knowledge[,] . . . questioning received ideas and perpetually revising traditional ways of thinking" (Graff, 1992, p. 7). In the language of hymnody, the church is to "tell the old, old story" while recognizing that "new occasions teach new duties."

Graff suggests that, rather than keeping the conflicted sides in separate corners or viewing the opposite position as a nuisance, we should view conflicts as the best sources for educating our constituencies and finding vitality in our subjects. In other words, what if this tug from two directions is not designed ever to be resolved? What if the creative tension between the conflicted sides is necessary to keep the conversation centered? What if the friction between sides is the fuel for new ideas?

Indeed, the conflicts of our culture war should be "energizing rather than paralyzing" (p. 43). Monologues preached to the polarized and secluded sides of disputes become dull and insipid, whereas dialogues with our adversaries give rise to new possibilities that challenge us to articulate clearly the faith within us.

Dialogues among Christians could then motivate the laity to learn scripture, theology, and history, and to integrate them with what they know through reason and experience. Such an exercise is a real and tangible motivation to study and grow, providing a much-needed boost for Christian education. Seen from this angle, dialogue focuses the educational offerings of the church, as members are challenged to engage adversaries on topics of deep importance.

Some will argue that there simply is not adequate time for church members to participate in substantive dialogue with their adversaries. This might be true if dialogue becomes simply one more program or activity to be added to our already crowded church and personal schedules. But the conflicts among Christians are all around us already, they are already on our minds, and they call for our best response of faith. In addition, the church is forever attempting to teach the Bible and theology to our sometimes indifferent congregations in a way that captures their imaginations and stirs them to deeper conviction and insight. Because conflicts exist within U.S. churches and time is limited, it is possible to blend existing activities such as Sunday school and other adult educational offerings with the need for spirited dialogue. These activities could take a variety of shapes:

- Neighboring churches on opposite sides of issues could pair up to meet on Sunday nights for a series of dialogues on a given topic. Even in the unlikely event that little substantive dialogue occurs, the opportunity for people simply to meet each other has an effect on the tone of dialogue and future interactions.

  For example, Joan Brown Campbell, general secretary of the National Council of Churches, and Pat Robertson of the Christian Broadcasting Network happened to meet at a 1995 gathering of U.S. religious leaders. These culture war adversaries were affected by this brief meeting. Campbell said she understood Robertson better; Robertson said their meeting would change the negative things they've said about each other. The two leaders also exchanged information.

- A spokesperson—lay or clergy—with a view that differs from the position of a particular church could speak to that church's Sunday school class or to an evening group. An interesting twist would be to ask the spokesperson to argue on behalf of the side of the host group, or for the visitor to hear and respond to the host group's attempt to articulate the visitor's side of the issue (Mouw, 1992, p. 56).

- Churches across the spectrum could sponsor community symposiums to allow various views to be voiced by their proponents, rather than asking a teacher or preacher to characterize, often inaccurately or cursorily, the basis for the other side's beliefs.

- A community of churches could organize a public round-table discussion, with a neutral, trained moderator, for a monthly dialogue session on relevant issues within the community. Participants could learn the skills and attitudes needed for constructive dialogue for use in this setting and in their local churches.

Graff's "teach the conflict" model does not come from a faith context, but his proposal will have a familiar ring to the ears of faith: Fear not. Take the risk of confronting one's adversary. Trust that truth will emerge from the open and frank exchange of ideas. Such an approach will sound uncomfortable to a culture that eschews conflict and praises gentility. Our preference is to smooth out the rough edges or to try to fix the problem. We resent the imposition of opposing opinions and are fearful when asked to defend our own positions. These old fears must be put away for dialogue to take place.

This "teach the conflict" model also recognizes the importance of granting space and respect for our adversaries. It assumes the appropriateness, even the necessity, of being in conflict over the issues that separate us in order to keep the church fresh and relevant for our day. It recognizes that truth has not taken up permanent residence on either side of the culture war. Truth transcends our sides.

Emotional Growth

Dialogue helps us grow up. Few other disciplines call for a higher level of emotional maturity than dialogue. Although some level of maturity is a prerequisite for dialogue, all participants grow emotionally in a variety of areas through the process of dialogue in at least some of the following ways:

- Dialogue forces us to deal with conflict rather than avoid or deny it. The tendency in our culture, and especially in the church, is to avoid conflict at all costs. Many of us have been taught to be nice, to engage in a respectable gentility that sidesteps direct conflict in favor of an indirect approach where one remains silent in the face of controversy and speaks later in the safety of one's comfort zone. In dialogue, participants are encouraged, even "required," to speak to the issues that divide them.

- Dialogue insists that participants put their feelings and beliefs into words. The only way an adversary can understand my hurts and hopes is if I find an adequate set of verbal images to paint a picture that conveys them. Naming and articulating feelings is a stretching, effortful exercise for many, especially males in our culture, who often aren't "in touch with their feelings" enough to put them into words. Dialogue relies on communication, so it sharpens participants' skills in finding and forming words. It does not accept the kind of stammering that too often substitutes for true communication, like the young woman who once said to me, "I don't know, it's just like . . . I don't know . . . you know?" I didn't know, and I asked her to do the difficult but necessary work of helping us both know more clearly by putting words to feelings.

- Dialogue cultivates honesty. It asks participants to explore the question, "What do I really believe and why?" This may be the first time that some participants have been challenged to reflect on the source of their beliefs. Once the exploration is completed, the next task is to be honest, both with oneself and the others in the dialogue.

- Dialogue asks us to be vulnerable before other people and to allow our beliefs to be informed by the community, including the adversary. Honest reflection and naming of one's rationale for beliefs can be a humbling, even embarrassing task. Our range of experience and knowledge is limited. Others see issues differently, with a different set of experiences and knowledge. In laying our views out for all to see and examine, most of us discover that our beliefs have developed from sources that are important but incomplete. In time, dialogue turns this self-revealing task from something we avoid to something we welcome.

- Dialogue teaches participants to be patient while an adversary says something they disagree with. Again, no easy task. Most of us are inclined to interrupt, correct, and rebut. It is a habit many people cultivate early, and one that is rewarded in circles of influence. Dialogue goes against the grain of modern communication patterns to encourage patience and careful listening that grow from an internal self-assurance that says, "I am not diminished by hearing out the views of others."

- Dialogue requires civility in the heat of a dispute. Emotions are explored and rechanneled, rather than allowed to take the easy outlet of counterattack.

- Dialogue resists the natural reaction to be defensive in the face of a perceived threat to one's views. It is human nature to be defensive. Dialogue disciplines our natural tendency toward defensiveness and channels it by asking what elicited the defensive feeling and using this insight as an occasion for growth, rather than simply letting it be an emotion that dislodges the dialogue. Dialogue monitors participants' reactions to opposing views by providing space for the participants to consider, "How am I feeling right now? Do I judge, accuse, and mentally argue with the speaker, or do I continue to employ my best thinking and listening?"

- Dialogue assumes that all mature participants will learn something new through the encounter. This assumption frees participants from feeling that they must have all the answers, or that a moment of insight must be squelched because it is somehow a threat to their position. The freedom to learn liberates participants to experiment with new ideas.

- Dialogue recognizes that the conflict is complex and on-going, and thus it will not be resolved quickly, or perhaps it may never be resolved, in the traditional sense of resolution. Participants grow beyond the typical quick-fix mentality to see that the ambiguity surrounding a conflict is where most of life is lived. Participants have permission to let go of the need to resolve the conflicts of life, even as they continue to confront the divisions that besiege them.

Dialogue can quell the rancorous battles fought within the church today. But that is only the beginning. Dialogue also is capable of transforming the church's conflicts into encounters of rich and profound growth. No other resource can promise such healing and hopeful results.

There is one key element to any successful dialogue: Someone has to see the possibilities in dialogue and get the ball rolling.

In Aesop's fable "The Mice in Council," the mice discuss what they should do to guard against their adversary, the cat. Several proposals were offered and rejected. Then a young mouse spoke: "I propose that we hang a bell around the cat's neck. Then wherever he approaches we shall hear him and be able to escape."

The young mouse sat down amidst tremendous applause. The idea was quickly made into a motion, seconded, and passed almost unanimously. Then an older mouse rose to his feet. "Friends, it takes a young mouse to come up with an idea so ingenious, and yet so simple. I have but one question to pose to the supporters of this plan: Which of you is going to bell the cat?" (1947, p. 13).

The notion of forming a dialogue within the church to confront our many areas of conflict may seem like trying to bell the cat—a good idea, but who is willing to take the risk?

You take it. God will be with you.

4

Establishing Ground Rules
for the Conversation

To dialogue is to join with people who have a different view from one's own on an issue in order to see what can be uncovered or learned together. It is turning one's adversary into a teammate to see what new things might break loose from a sustained conversation on a particular subject.

The forms taken by such an interchange vary widely. A few dialogues have the term "dialogue" specifically affixed to the conversation even before it begins. As we will see, this form of dialogue can be planned, publicized, and regulated. Ground rules can be laid out and agreed on before the conversation ensues, and the exchange can last for an evening, a weekend, or over an extended period of time. These more formal dialogues serve an important role in helping large groups work through issues that have paralyzed their communication and thwarted their witness.

Other dialogues are spontaneous, one-time conversations that occur at a holiday family gathering, within a Sunday school class, or in a leadership meeting. They arise in the course of conversation or in the process of doing church business. Participants are not prepared in advance. No ground rules are set forth; the only ground rules or preparation are those unspoken rules that govern the course of most civil conversation, or as will be suggested, the guidelines and techniques taught in a local church or association of churches during a time of relative peace and tranquility.

Still other dialogues, although informal, are more sustained in length—either a single, lengthy dialogue or a series of conversations over a period of time on a point of disagreement. As the dialogue lengthens, the intensity decreases, and the pace is more peaceful and welcoming. One student of dialogue suggests that, at its best, dialogue is a "continued, thoughtful exchange about the things that most matter. It is time to sit under the apple tree together and talk, without time pressures. It is the kind of conversation that we have forgotten in the pace of western, modern life" (Brown, 1995). This form of dialogue will be recognized as such only in retrospect, having employed the tools necessary to constitute a meaningful deliberation of issues between parties with substantive disagreements. Although this form of dialogue doesn't make the evening news, it is a more prevalent form of dialogue and has a quiet but powerful impact on the life and health of the church, both local and global.

Formal and informal dialogues look and feel different from each other. However, both forms of dialogue are recognized as such when they employ the unique dialogue principles represented by the Ten Guidelines for Dialogue first listed in Chapter Three. As we elaborate on these guidelines here, we see the various forms of dialogue as well as various techniques that aid them.

Risk

> We will face our differences. We will consider all views and information, even if they conflict with our basic assumptions about the issue and result in conclusions that differ from our own.

Any dialogue has an element of risk to it. The essence of dialogue comes from the willingness to lay out one's deeply held convictions before the other dialogue participants in a way that leaves these convictions temporarily unprotected and vulnerable. A participant in a dialogue on women in ministry suggested that this dimension of the dialogue process "feels like laying a naked, defenseless child in the middle of a football field with a game in progress." As a pro-choice advocate put it, "How do I know what the other side will do if I acknowledge, for example, that the thought of late-term abortions is disgusting to me? They'll jump on that admission like hungry sharks. And they'll draw all kinds of conclusions that simply aren't true." A proponent of banning certain books from public schools acknowledged, "I wanted to say that I thought our side had gone a bit overboard with the list of books. Some of them I didn't find personally offensive. But to say this [in a dialogue] would have broken our unified front. It also would have made me look stupid, since I've been pushing for restrictions on books for so long."

· · · · · · · ·

The risk of losing ground, metaphorically and literally, was on the minds of two groups that shared a property on which they ran parallel, but unrelated, retreat programs. The programs were vastly different in style. One group appealed to more liberal people who responded to creative methods of prayer, meditation techniques, and worship. The other group was traditional in theology and methodology. The first group was led by a younger staff, while the second group had older leaders who had been at their jobs for many years. Over time, significant resentment had built up between the groups so that the groups no longer talked to each other. Each group stereotyped the other—the traditional group was characterized as "God's frozen chosen," and the contemporary group was categorized as "the touchy-feely circus." An underlying tension permeated the retreat center and was felt by visitors. Eventually the animosity between the groups became so strong that the arrangement of sharing a camp ground no longer seemed possible.

Someone proposed a dialogue. They agreed on a facilitator who made one condition: that those who participated in the dialogue would have to release the need for a specific outcome to the process. Instead, they should be open to what the Spirit would do. This felt extremely risky for all involved, especially the people from the traditional retreat group: What if we are belittled or told that our ways are wrong and need correction? What if the other side tries to take over our program? With considerable fear, all agreed to this condition for dialogue.

Rather than address the issue head-on, the facilitator invited participants to share their life experiences by describing themselves in several ways: on a personal level, through the roles and titles they fill, and through the historical and cultural contexts in which they have been shaped. After sharing this information with the group, participants were asked, "In the conflict before us, what is the highest value that you are attempting to honor? And what is the truth that you attempt to live out of?"

After everyone responded, participants were invited to ask questions of each other. They asked about each other's methods and their underlying assumptions, such as "How do things like dance, artwork, and massage relate to spirituality?" or "What meaning do you find in liturgies from the past?" As participants asked, then listened deeply, they gradually began to see the conflict not simply from their own experience, but also from the other side's perspective. In doing so, a common ground became visible between them— good, important ground. In fact, they realized, both groups do love God deeply. Both groups do want to be faithful to the Spirit of God. Both groups believe deeply in the mystery and efficacy of prayer. And, though they had different expressions of faithfulness, both groups moved to a place where they could express admiration and respect for the other side.

Said one of the traditional leaders, "When I see you doing outdoor prayer rituals at night, it looks and feels like Halloween to me. But as I think of it in light of your cultural experience—the generation you grew up in and the way you seem more connected to the earth and the cosmos—it begins to make sense."

A leader from the innovative worship leaders responded, "When I see your traditional expressions of worship it feels so dead and meaningless to me. It even feels a little bit evil. It reminds me of going to church as a kid, when my mother made me and I hated it.

God was boring and mean. But when you talk about it, I hear it as
something incredibly life-giving for you. I realize how deeply it con-
nects with your upbringing and your love of the church of your
youth. The tradition feeds your soul in a way that it doesn't feed
mine. Maybe it's not so bad after all . . . although I still don't choose
to worship in that style!"

From the vantage point of the common ground, the issues that
previously were impasses had dissolved. One participant noted,
"The issues that divided us were no longer so emotionally charged.
The conflict kind of fell away." A renewed sense of compassion
arose for those who had been adversaries, and a new appreciation
developed for the contribution each retreat style played in meeting
the needs of people in the church. Ultimately, the two groups not
only were able to co-exist, but began discussions on the benefits of
operating as two streams of a single retreat center. In preparing for
these discussions, they discovered that this was precisely the origin
of their two groups thirty years earlier: A traditional retreat program
had established a newer expression to meet the diverse needs of the
church.

Respect

> We will cultivate respect for our dialogue partners as human
> beings and as fellow Christians. We will take each other's
> views and convictions seriously. We will not question one
> another at the point of sincerity or Christian commitment.

Stereotypes are rarely, if ever, overcome by theory. Rather, it is
through relationships that people are able to embrace some dimension of the other side that was previously abhorrent or unknown to
them. The disagreements may remain, but through respect and relationships the polarization between people is softened, the various,
subtle shades of meaning are allowed to enter in and inform the
conversation. I may still think your position is wrong, just as I did
before the dialogue, but now I see your position growing from

underlying assumptions that you hold deeply and sincerely. I can no longer dismiss you as being merely unchristian or irrational.

．．．．．．．

For example, one day a pastor received an angry phone call that developed into a kind of dialogue. The previous day, on the eve of the first execution in his state in many years, the pastor was quoted in the local news as opposing capital punishment. The caller identified himself by name, told the pastor what church he attended, then said, "I just don't see how you can call yourself a Christian if you take that stand. The Bible clearly supports capital punishment in Leviticus. Don't you believe in the Bible?" He continued to talk in this vein for several minutes. "You're just trying to saddle up to the liberal media," he accused. The pastor listened carefully, responding when the caller paused, presumably to hear a response from him. "That is a valid point," said the pastor, "and one that is certainly important in the question of capital punishment. This is obviously a critical issue for you."

"It would be for you too if your daughter had been killed by someone who's on death row today," shouted the caller. His voice level decreased. "There hasn't been an hour in the nine years since she died that I haven't thought of her. She would have been thirty this year."

Later, the pastor reflected, "That piece of information changed my whole response to the caller. Frankly, I assumed he was just another old fundamentalist law-and-order guy that wanted to fix the world by killing off the bad people. His call reminded me of the complexity of the issue, especially for people like him, for whom capital punishment is not an ideological question but a part of his everyday existence."

As the conversation continued, the pastor offered his own position, both personally and biblically, while intentionally avoiding a battle of scriptures. "My position against capital punishment comes from the way I understand that Jesus calls me to act and react in our world," he said, but he also went on to acknowledge his own discomfort with where his faith led him on this issue. "Of course, that leaves us with the question of what is an appropriate consequence for murder," he admitted.

The two talked for twenty minutes. The caller argued with the pastor's position, but eventually quit using terms like "liberal" and "bleeding hearts" and began to concede that the issue was more complex than he cared to admit. He even laughed when the pastor noted that the "liberal media" that he allegedly was playing to was critical of the stance he had taken against abortion. "I guess that's true," said the caller. By the end, the two men were thinking together, raising the strengths and weaknesses in their positions. When the conversation came to a close, the caller said, "I want to thank you for listening to me and taking me seriously. A lot of people wouldn't have given me the time of day. You've given me a new perspective that I hadn't seen before."

• • • • • • • •

Sometimes the respect between adversaries is so low that dialogue is impossible. Respect must be rebuilt, or built for the first time, in order for dialogue to be possible. An example of this kind of foundational building in action is seen in the work of the Interfaith Health Program (IHP), a program of the Carter Center. IHP is based on the conviction that religious groups do not get far by starting with a discussion of their points of disagreement. As IHP director, Gary Gunderson, notes, "There are good reasons why sincere people of faith see things differently, why worship differs, why there are different expectations of God's action in this life and beyond. This is why interfaith dialogue frequently is conducted tenderly and often abstractly. These discussions tend to find an inoffensive least-common-denominator that is so lacking in substance as to be powerless, even boring" (n.d., p. 22).

In light of this realization, IHP calls on a common element within our faith communities to unite us: the ethic to care for the needy, the sick, and the poor. IHP believes that if churches respond to the common call to action from our faith traditions and commit to work together, the result will be a new source of energy and a reason and a context to talk together. Dialogue, if it happens at all, takes place *after* a commitment is made to the very practical, primary business of united ministry. Dialogue becomes a side benefit to working together. Out of this shared ministry comes the subsequent need to know and respect our new co-laborers. "You can't respect someone you don't understand. You can't understand someone you haven't listened to. You can't listen to someone you haven't spent time with" (Gunderson, n.d., p. 18).

This model is one of collaboration first, dialogue second. It assumes that if conflicted groups (such as white and black, liberal and conservative) join together to fight a common enemy (such as poverty), they will ultimately build respect between the groups, move beyond the paralysis brought on by their former win-lose competition, and provide an environment in which to dialogue substantively about their differences in the future.

Fairness

> We will not judge people on the other side by popular stereotypes or by their least admirable expressions. We will allow people to define themselves, rather than presuming to know them from inference, categorization, or outside observation. We will allow those on the other side the freedom to restate, change, or expand their position in the course of the dialogue without interpreting these actions as a sign of weakness, confusion, or ambivalence.

We are all prone to stereotyping, often without being aware of it. Stereotyping helps us feel we understand others and can anticipate how and why others think and act. When we stereotype, we categorize others based on our subjective and selective assessment of external information. We generalize people and issues in a way that ignores exceptions, ambiguity, and alternative ideas. Stereotyping is inherently dishonest and destructive to dialogue.

Within the church, for example, people on the Right are carica-tured as "poor, uneducated and easy to command," as a Washington Post writer alleged (quoted in Marty, 1995). They are depicted as ostriches who stick their heads in the sand, who refuse to confront the ambiguities of life because their world view is too simplistic to deal with them. They are stereotyped as strict, angry, Bible-thumpers, homophobics, people who care about the unborn but not the living, military hawks, and people without a social conscience.

People on the Left are labeled "radical individualists" or "secu-lar humanists." They are depicted as worldly, ungodly, wishy-washy, apathetic, indifferent, trendy, liberal, even demonic. In describing the Right's conflict with the Left, James Dobson characterized the left as evil: "We are engaged in a battle—not primarily with our philosophical opponents—but against 'Satan, who leads the whole world astray' (Rev. 12:9)" (1995, p. 28).

This method of framing an issue is standard fare in motion pic-tures; audiences are led to view one side as nice, decent, and well-meaning, just like us, while the other side is characterized as mean, despicable, and sadistic. Thus viewers are encouraged to identify with the good guys and disown the bad guys. No ambiguity exists. The bad guys are simply bad; how they got that way, or why they act the way they act is not part of the script. This allows the movie to flow nicely toward an awaited climax where good triumphs, the bad guys are vanquished without regrets, and viewers leave with the reassurance that all's right with the world.

Dialogue recognizes that life is never this clear or free from ambiguity. It moves us beyond stereotypes to understand and respect the legitimate, undergirding views of the other side. To help in this process of de-stereotyping, the Common Ground Network designed a group dialogue exercise to explore stereotypes applied to partici-pants of the issue in question and to separate the true elements of the stereotypes from the false elements. Each side creates a list of assumptions, stereotypes, beliefs, and attitudes that they think the other side applies to them. When the lists are shared, participants are asked, "Is there something in the stereotypes you've listed that is particularly painful or inaccurate?" or "What do you never want said about you again?" Participants are encouraged to share their experiences in a way that would help people understand, describing their feelings, using a sentence such as "When I hear the phrase ____, I feel ____."

Participants are then asked, "Looking at the lists you created, is there an assumption or stereotype that is true about you, at least in part?" Put another way, "Which of these statements is fair to say about you?" Participants then review the list created by the other side, which denotes the stereotypes they face, and the participants are asked, "Do you relate to what is there? Is there anything that stirs strong feelings in you?"

Finally, the entire group considers common ideas or reactions to stereotypes and considers implications for how they will talk about the other side outside of the dialogue. (See Appendix for more on the Common Ground Network).

Another technique that is useful for addressing stereotypes and attitudes is called Role-Reversal Interviews. People are interviewed in front of the group, pretending to hold the view opposite from their own and speaking from its perspective. When the interview is completed, people who actually hold this view are asked for evaluation and clarification.

Caution is necessary, not only to avoid explicit stereotypes that put down participants on the other side, but also to be aware of how a particular tone, attitude, or tactic is perceived. For example, in a dialogue that came out of a conflict between a church governing board and a women's group within the church, one of the women said that a decision of the board made her feel scolded or criticized. A man on the board quickly explained to the woman that she was not being criticized and should not feel that way since that was not what was intended. He went on to explain the rationale of the board. He made no stereotypical remarks, nor did he use a condescending tone of voice. But because he assumed the woman didn't know all the facts and because he took on the role of teaching and correcting her, and because she was already feeling dismissed and hurt, her reaction was surprisingly explosive: "It just lit the conversation like gasoline," said the facilitator. "All this anger poured out from the women. The leaders didn't know what they had done to make the women angry, so they quickly tried to quell the situation by trying in a very reasonable way to tell and explain the situation further to the women, which simply added fuel to the fire, until the dialogue began to fall apart."

At that point, the skilled observer to the dialogue recognized what was happening and suggested that the group stop for a moment, sit in silence, and notice the dynamics of the conversation—how the pace of the speaking had picked up, how voices had grown louder and higher, how people were making statements about others, and how they were trying to persuade others of their views rather than sharing their own questions and assumptions. The goal for this pause in the dialogue (which became a kind of dialogue within the dialogue) was to help the group identify where it had stopped talking in mutual dialogue and had begun talking in other-directed statements, that is, statements aimed at what the other party had done to impair the dialogue.

The group was then asked to share what assumptions they had made about the statements they'd heard—that is, they reoriented the conversation by using such lines as "When you said ___, I said to myself, 'Here is what that means:___.'" When these assumptions were aired, those who made the statements were able to either affirm or clarify the assumptions or apologize. For example, one of the women said, "I came to the dialogue anticipating that our concerns would be dismissed as trivial, so I was set to detonate the moment I heard someone imply that we didn't know what we were talking about. When you said, 'Your feelings are ill-founded,' I heard you saying, 'You don't know what you're talking about.'"

On the other side, one of the male leaders apologized for taking on the teaching role of explaining the women's feelings to them.

He admitted that the conflict made him uncomfortable emotionally and that being logical was his way of trying to put out the fire and pacify the situation. In being honest and vulnerable with the women about his own discomfort, trust was rebuilt between the groups, and the dialogue was resumed.

Humility

We acknowledge that our understanding of God and the ways of God is limited and finite. We recognize that issues requiring dialogue are often complex and ambiguous, even when they appear straightforward from one particular vantage point, and that no one has a final answer to the question at hand. We will avoid the presumption of oversimplification.

Humility is a key to dialogue. The old human habits of win-lose slip into a dialogue to thwart it at the point of humility. But dialogue is not a contest to see who has the most impressive statistics or the greatest amount of data. Thus, dialogue refuses to elevate certain participants based on their position, title, academic credentials, or any other external expression of power. Dialogue requires equal footing, where, in humility, people work together with adversaries to learn from each other and to search for new levels of truth on a point of disagreement.

And yet humility may be the most difficult dimension of dialogue for Christians who are adamant enough about their beliefs to interact with those of opposing views. This is especially true for pastors and other leaders to whom parishioners or group members look for guidance and direction. Leaders are expected to exude confidence in their views, enough so that they can lead a group to act on them. This level of confidence leaves little room for the kind of humility that says, "I don't know all there is to know about this subject. There may be additional information or a different angle to this subject that is equally valid, that may be more accurate than my view, or may even contradict my view."

Humility is a doctrinal difficulty for people on the Right. Dialogue's open-ended stance that welcomes new insight can feel unfaithful for people whose theology is more closed and contained. If all light and truth are to be found in the pages of the Bible, then it seems inconsistent to some on the Right to say that we don't know all there is to know about God. (This idea will be explored further in Chapter Five.)

People on the Left can share this difficulty with humility, not because their doctrinal position discourages it, but because they presume that the Right has nothing to offer. A self-described liberal told of his hesitation when he was invited to attend a local Promise Keepers gathering. "I knew these guys were not very savvy intellectually, and assumed that they'd roast me for dinner when they found out I was a stay-at-home dad, the husband of a Methodist minister, and a vegetarian! And yet I felt a need to be with some other guys—a need that wasn't being met in my own church. So I went. What I found were guys like me who cared about their families and who wanted to be good husbands and fathers. I also found that these guys could very humbly and earnestly go to God for guidance and peace in a way that I'd long since abandoned. Their faith was real and powerful. In a way, they brought me back to a deep faith in God. We still have major disagreements over social issues and some theology, but it's not the most important part of the gathering."

Teamwork

We will work together as partners with those on the other side of the issue in order to learn something new about our own position, their position, or a new position yet to be discovered.

In a work such as this one on dialogue, it might be helpful to contextualize such terms as "other side," "enemy," "adversary," and "opponent" by using quotation marks as a way to remind the reader that, once dialogue has begun, these terms are no longer accurate. Up to the point of the dialogue, these terms may be helpful for identification purposes. But once a dialogue, formal or informal, commences, these terms can hide the fact that we are on the same team, working together to search for truth. A company negotiator said, during a particularly divisive point in a dialogue with union representatives, "There is no other side," as he stood and moved his chair to the union side of the table; "We're all on the same side! We've got to solve this together!"

One participant who caught the real nature and possibilities of dialogue explained, "If my commitment is to the truth, which I recognize is always beyond the limits of my sight, then I need, through dialogue, to see more accurately by learning about what someone else sees and experiences about the truth. If, on the other hand, my commitment is only to the truth as I now understand it, then dialogue is a threat rather than an aid to my being a person of truth."

Physicist David Bohm, whose writings provide a philosophical underpinning for much of the work done on dialogue today, saw the need for teamwork to get behind the assumptions, polarized opinions, and ineffective ways we deal with conflict. It is not possible to reach these fundamental issues in isolation; rather, it requires the teamwork of conversation, a dialogue, to reach what Bohm (1985) calls "collective mindfulness."

Dialogue recognizes that our enemy is not simply a problem to be solved, but part of the solution, and without this enemy there would be no solution. It is not enough for my side to win; our former enemy must become part of the new creation. As Martin Luther King, Jr., said of the civil rights movement and the infamous Alabama sheriff who blocked marchers with guard dogs and fire hoses, "We have not succeeded until Bull Conner is part of the solution." Solution, as defined by dialogue, is not a particular outcome, but a process of living with and managing the conflicting convictions represented by dialogue participants.

Jim Wallis, who has worked to raise a faith-based voice in the politics of our country, understands the need for both sides in the church's recent splits to come together as a team. As Wallis looks at the church, he sees that the Left speaks to social oppression as it relates to social injustice and the need for just social systems, whereas the Right speaks to cultural breakdown as it relates to a collapse of values and the need for personal responsibility. Wallis believes that "social oppression and cultural breakdown are the twin signs of our age" (1994, p. 9), and that *both* signs of our age are real and connected. Faithful response is not a matter of either-or, but rather both-and. We need Christians who are currently fighting against one of the twin signs of our age to team up in dialogue with other Christians who are fighting against the other twin, rather than opposing each other on the issues.

Teamwork recognizes the Biblical notion that, despite our profound differences, Christians in conflict are on the same side. The fact that we are on the same team is non-negotiable. The question is, How will we relate to our estranged teammates? Will we fight for the relationship or against it? Will we fight to preserve our union or to destroy it? Will we fight to solve the problem or to salve our egos? Are we committed to the relationship, or to feeling good simply by eliminating unpleasantness?

Teamwork sounds good in theory but is often difficult in practice. Peter Senge reminds us that "no matter how committed people are to a shared vision, they still are steeped in the habits of game playing. . . . " (1990, p. 276). Rhetoric about dialogue cannot hide the fact that human beings are far more skilled in contests that presume winners and losers and that reward those who are aggressive, dexterous, cunning, and elusive. Besides, let's be honest: There is a part of us that loves a contest—it gets our blood boiling!

These old habits die hard. We've been playing these games since Jacob outfoxed Esau. But the skills used for these old games are counterproductive to dialogue. For dialogue to take place within the Christian community, we need to unlearn old habits and retool ourselves for a new way of relating. We must be schooled in the spirit and hope of dialogue.

Teamwork calls for participants to keep in mind that their adversaries-teammates are also people with feelings that can be touched and affected. They are not robots or *Star Trek*'s Mr. Spock, with no sensitivity to statements that belittle or criticize. When the dialogue is in danger because your adversary-teammate has been wounded by what was said, work from your end to restore the conversation by reframing the hurtful statement, whether or not the hurt was intended. For example, when you feel yourself responding negatively to another person in dialogue, you might say, "This may be more my problem than yours, but when you said [restate speaker's words], I felt [describe feelings]. Am I misunderstanding what you said or intended?" Or when someone expresses a strong view that seems to come out of nowhere, you might say, "You may be right, but I'd like to understand more. What leads you to believe . . . ?" (Senge and others, 1994).

Openness

> We will be open about the nature of our disagreement and will test our assumptions about where the points of disagreement are. We will not judge the correctness or orthodoxy of a position solely by how it relates to our own position.

Dialogue hones and clarifies the essential issues of disagreement, which is crucial for effective communication to take place. When we presume to know the full nature of a conflict, we risk missing entirely the essential point or points of concern.

For example, in her work on abortion, Frederica Mathewes-Green discovered through dialogue that pro-choice proponents have a range of rationales behind their stance. "For some it is the fear that 'unwanted' children will be abused; for others it is the specter of deaths from illegal abortions; still others may be concerned about overpopulation. I learned that a pro-life approach that insists 'It's a baby!' may be answering a question none are asking and missing the question they are [asking]" (1998, p. 28). This information has been vital to her in helping redefine the points that need to be brought out in future conversations on the abortion conflict.

Openness in dialogue also requires participants to temporarily suspend judgment of the veracity of statements made by others during the dialogue. Rather than assuming they know what is being said or whether a statement is accurate, participants take a wait-and-see attitude. They monitor their reactions and use what they feel to help raise questions that allow the dialogue to uncover hidden concerns. For example, when a statement evokes a feeling of defensiveness in a participant, rather than reacting to the statement, the dialogue participant expresses what is being felt so that the group can uncover the source of the feeling. A skilled facilitator (or skilled participants in an informal dialogue) asks, "What do you assume when you hear this statement?" or "Where does this statement touch you personally?"

A veteran of Baptist conflicts recognized the essential element to openness and checking our assumptions: "If I say, 'I don't believe the Bible is literally true,' you may hear me saying, 'Darwin is right, we're all monkeys and there is no God.' If we can learn together what my statement triggers in you, then we can begin to talk. In fact, I may believe as much as you that there is a God who is active and powerful in creation, who is worthy of worship, and who sent Jesus to this world. It's just the mechanism by which God is revealed through the Bible that is different."

The process of examining assumptions, meaning, jumps in logic, and conclusions—those of others as well as our own—is a key ingredient to dialogue. Unfortunately, examining one's own assumptions is extremely difficult. It is difficult to be objective about the beliefs that one holds as fundamentally true and irrefutable. It is even more difficult to be conscious of the mental processes we use in selecting the data and drawing the conclusions on which we think and act. Still more difficult is determining someone else's assumptions and conclusions.

For example, Connie picked up an interesting-looking brochure on an upcoming retreat to be led by a counselor in the church. She had been wanting to take a retreat for some time. But as she reviewed the brochure, Connie's eyes stopped on the phrase "God reveals Godself to us. . . . " in one of the workshop descriptions. This phrase reminded her of a friend, Tina, who is involved in women's issues. In Connie's opinion, Tina had gone overboard in her concerns about equality for woman. If the brochure uses the same language as her friend, it must mean that the retreat would share her friend's agenda. The retreat, therefore, must be liberal, feminist, and political. With that, Connie tossed the brochure in the trash.

Connie had unknowingly climbed each step on the "ladder of inference" (Figure 4.1). This precarious ladder, developed by Chris Argyris and used in *The Fifth Discipline Fieldbook* (Senge and others, 1994), charts the erroneous course of assumption-building that often foils the process of dialogue: we select certain observable facts from a host of facts. We then interpret these selected facts and add our own spin to them. We draw conclusions, based on our interpretations, and formulate beliefs about the situation. We receive and interpret future information and base our actions on these beliefs.

In Connie's case, a phrase ("God reveals Godself to us . . . ") is lifted from an entire brochure and connected with the language of Tina, who is unrelated to the retreat. Based on experience with Tina, Connie assumes that the retreat has a certain politically correct agenda that Connie finds unattractive. She concludes that the retreat will promote the same agenda that Tina does, and believes that this must be the agenda of the entire church. "I need to look for a new church," she says as she discards the brochure.

Had Connie been open to the realization that she had made some significant jumps in logic, she might have been willing to stop and check out some of her assumptions. She might have discovered, for example, that the writer of the brochure, a counselor, had a legitimate reason for using "Godself" in place of a male term for God, such as "Himself": this counselor hears people who've had negative experiences with men say that the use of male pronouns for God colors their experience of God and discourages them from pursuing

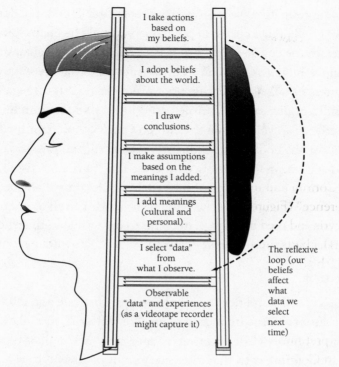

Figure 4.1. Ladder of Inference.
From *The Fifth Discipline Fieldbook* by Peter Senge, Charlotte Roberts et al. Copyright © 1994 by Peter M. Senge, Art Kleiner, Charlotte Roberts, Richard B. Ross and Bryan J. Smith. Used by permission of Doubleday, a division of Bantam Doubleday Dell Publishing Group, Inc.

a life of faith. Beyond that, there was no specific feminist agenda to the retreat; that was a concoction in Connie's mind.

It is clear to see how the ladder of inference affects the dialogue process. As Mathewes-Green observed, "When we say, 'Abortion is an immoral choice because it kills a baby,' [pro-choice proponents] hear, 'People who favor abortion are immoral people.' I had long wondered why, at debates, I would attack abortion, and my opponent would not defend abortion but attack me" (1998, p. 29).

The rungs on the ladder of inference are well-worn. It is a normal and necessary part of life to infer meaning in our experiences and in information we receive. Thus, openness in dialogue does not ask us to eliminate our assumptions—that would be impossible—but rather, in the course of the dialogue, to reflect on our assumptions to see if we have taken some steps in inference that were based on incorrect or unbalanced assumptions. We can do this through direct or indirect questions: Connie could have asked a church leader directly, "Can you tell me the church's position on feminist theology?," or she could have indirectly asked, "What does the phrase 'God-self' mean?" or "I noticed you used the phrase 'God-self. . . .'"

Since openness is one of the criteria for healthy dialogue, partners acknowledge their own jumps in logic, as well as encourage others to make their steps of inference more visible so that they can be mutually examined and explored.

Listening

> We will stand next to people on the other side and attempt to hear the issue from their place. We will avoid formulating our response while another is speaking. We will attempt to empathize with the other side's point of view.

Listening is a tangible way to communicate value to another person, particularly an adversary. It calls dialogue participants to set aside any tendency to dominate conversations or to be the center of attention. Instead of following our usual tendency to talk, participants earnestly listen to others, taking a vibrant interest in what motivates the other side, how they see and respond to the world, what feeds their souls and forms their values. Scott Peck calls this "bracketing," to temporarily give up or set aside one's own prejudices, frames of reference, and desires in order to experience, as far as possible, the speaker's world from the inside, stepping inside his or her shoes (1978, pp. 127–128).

But let's be honest: listening is time-consuming and effortful. Far easier and more natural is the attitude that "because you disagree with me, you are a problem to be fixed rather than a person to be heard."

This is especially true when we feel responsible for playing a certain role, like the parents at a restaurant with their small daughter who said to the server, "I'll have a hot dog, French fries, and a milkshake." The parents smiled at the server and said, "She'll have the turkey, rice, and green beans." When the server came back with the hot dog, fries, and shake, the little girl beamed, "Wow! She treated me like a person!" Leaders who represent certain positions—pastors, agency staff, or laity invested in a cause—often find that their habit of playing and defending a certain role makes listening difficult.

Another detriment to listening is the human reaction of defensiveness. Defensiveness is natural in the midst of dialogue. When I feel attacked or believe my position is being threatened, I revert to what some call "reptilian thinking," that is, thinking that emanates from a more primal, reactive part of my brain. When an object is propelled toward my face, my hands go up in an unconscious reaction to the threat. Similarly, when I feel my position threatened on the issue in question, I react with a defensive move such as diverting or sabotaging the conversation, counterattacking, or hiding behind the views of experts.

Defensiveness may be natural, but it hinders the kind of careful listening that can yield understanding and empathy. In times of conflict, listening becomes a way to find a loophole in the adversary's views, to gather ammunition, or to formulate an offensive response. The participant is no longer listening at this point, but preparing for battle, waiting for a chance to seize control of the conversation by reclaiming the role of speaker. The precocious Calvin of Bill Watterson's "Calvin and Hobbes" cartoon typifies this in a conversation with Hobbes, his mild-mannered tiger. "When a person pauses mid-sentence to choose a word, that's the best time to jump in and change the subject!" said Calvin excitedly. "It's like an interception in football! You grab the other guy's idea and run the opposite way with it! The more sentences you complete, the higher your score. The idea is to block the other guy's thoughts and express your own. That's how you win!"

Hobbes observes, "Conversations aren't contests."

"OK. A point for you," says Calvin with a frown. "But I'm still ahead."

Sensitive speakers who pick up on this ploy on the "listener's" part feel cheated and minimized and will retreat to safety. One technique that keeps participants from competing for the floor and encourages more listening is to set a rule that only one person may speak at a time. The speaker must hold a certain object—a designated Bible or a carpet sample (to symbolize "having the floor")—which is held until the thought is completed. Then the speaker relinquishes the object to someone else who has indicated a desire to speak or returns it to the center of the room. The group is invited to playfully help monitor if someone else speaks out of turn or tries to finish someone else's thought ("Hey, who has the floor?"). This simple tool provides freedom for speakers to pause between sentences or ideas before continuing to speak. It also provides space between speakers for silence and reflection so that ideas can be fully considered.

Although no technique can substitute for the basic task of careful listening, there are occasions when exercises for facilitating a dialogue, such as having the speaker hold a Bible or piece of carpet, are necessary and effective. The following dialogue exercises come from *Mediation and Facilitation Training Manual*, an invaluable resource compiled by the Mennonite Conciliation Service (see Appendix).

> *Interview*. Select a few capable representatives from each side of the issue for an interview in front of the group. The interviewer should be as neutral as possible and should conduct the interview in an informal manner, offering a paraphrase of what is said for clarity, as needed. After all interviews are conducted, ask others if there is another view that has not been represented.
>
> *Introductions*. Persons on opposite sides talk one-on-one, and then each introduces the other person,

describing briefly where they stand on the issue at hand and why. The person who was introduced has a chance to clarify the introduction that has been made, if necessary (Stutzman and Schrock-Schenk, 1995, p. 214).

These techniques invite listening. But listening—hearing what another person says and considering it carefully—calls for not only being attentive to the words of another person, but also making a place within oneself where the words can be received with openness.

• • • • • • •

Members of a Baptist church were deeply divided over a proposal to modify their bylaws in order to receive members whose believer's baptism was not done by immersion. "This is such a minor, trivial issue," said the group advocating the change. "We're just talking about a quantity of water, not the theology behind the baptism. Anyone who would exclude a person based on the quantity of water used at their baptism is straining at gnats."

As the dialogue slowly moved people to the deeper concerns underlying the presenting issue, the advocates of a bylaw change heard other members speak of their concern that the church was slipping from its Baptist roots and abandoning traditions, such as immersion baptism, that were among the distinctive traits of being Baptist. They saw such a move as a repudiation of the past, and a abandonment of saints depicted in the church's windows, who had been persecuted for their views on baptism. It became clearer, through listening, that the issue before the church was far more than the quantity of water—it was the church's history and self-understanding.

Interestingly, the advocates of change who had listened carefully to the members of the other side were the ones who were first able to verbalize for the group the deeper, more complex issues behind the surface issue. This not only focused the group on the more important issue, but also gave people who resisted the change a sense that they were valued and respected. One person from that group said, "When someone from the other side said what I was feeling better than I could have said it, even though she didn't agree with it, I felt like we were working together. It also made me want to listen more carefully to their point of view."

First-Person Speech

We will limit our speaking to the information, materials, and evidence we have available to us. We will focus on how we can deepen our understanding of the other side and narrow the gap from our side, rather than worry or complain about what the other party will or will not do.

Many of us are tired of the Rogerian style of counseling that mimics the speaker with "what I hear you saying" language. We are also suspicious of slightly modified accusations that are put in "I-message" form ("I feel that you are a bigoted idiot."). This is not the true nature of first-person speech. To speak in first-person is to own one's prejudices and assumptions. It is to speak of what you know and feel and, through dialogue, to uncover the nature of your thinking, both for yourself and for your adversary.

The following interchange is from a formal dialogue session of a congregation split over use of church funds. The difficulty people have speaking in first-person mode is illustrated, along with the process of forming first-person speech.

CHURCH MEMBER: The building committee gets whatever money it wants, while our committees have to wait to see what is left over.

FACILITATOR: Let's explore your statement. Your concern is that there is an inequity when it comes to distributing the church's money that is based on a decision or a policy that you've been unable to find. Is that correct?

CHURCH MEMBER: I suppose so. As far as I know, there is no policy. They just decide things arbitrarily.

FACILITATOR: So your concern is to find out if there is a policy for distributing funds so that it can be reviewed to make sure it is equitable.

CHURCH MEMBER: That's right. I want to know how things are decided, because from where I sit, it doesn't seem fair.

FACILITATOR: That's a legitimate question. (To the group:) Who has information on how the church disbursed funds in the last year? And if there is a priority list for disbursements, what group would be responsible for making such a policy? Would that group be willing to come back to our next session? . . .

The facilitator helped focus the question and put it in the form of a statement that spoke to the real issue of concern, rather than a statement filled with accusation and assumption. She did not rule out the statement or disallow it because it included accusation and assumption; rather, she guided the church member to get to the heart of the issue, both in terms of the feelings the member had as well as the question that needed to be answered.

Throughout this dialogue, each time someone made an assumption or a generalization, the facilitator would subtly halt the process in order to reframe the statement, unpack all the assumptions, make a plan for getting the concrete information needed to test the assumption, and at the same time acknowledge the larger, underlying feelings that had given birth to the statement.

Gradually, people began to use I-statements: "I don't understand why this happens" or "I am concerned about that." Then the group participated in unpacking both the presenting concern and the underlying concerns until the person who made the generalization felt some sense of satisfaction.

An approach that encourages first-person speech from the outset of dialogue has been developed by the Public Conversations Project (PCP). PCP was founded by a group of family therapists who noticed similarities between families at an impasse and groups engaged in polarized debate. "Those on each side believe they hold the high moral ground and are prey to unprovoked attacks from the other side, which they see as power hungry, self-centered, destructive, and perhaps even deranged. Each side enlists bands of allies to support its own interpretation of history. The opponents' interactions are almost ritualized, and their strife, although costly, resists resolution" (Chasin and Herzig, 1994, p. 150). On the other hand, as with family counseling, when the group breaks through an impasse and has a truly new conversation, understanding and creative options become possible.

PCP discovered that the approach they used with families could also be used with groups divided over public issues. Over time, PCP has developed ways to foster constructive exchange by creating a safe setting and a structured format in which people can speak and listen in new ways about what divides them. The aim is not agreement or a resolution, but a humanizing of the individuals on the opposing sides.

PCP has facilitated dialogue on a variety of issues using a variety of formats. The particular model presented here was developed for conducting introductory dialogues on abortion. It is generally used with groups of six participants, three who identify themselves as pro-life and three who identify themselves as pro-choice, who come together for one evening. Participants are recruited through mailings and flyers and by word of mouth. People who express an interest receive a detailed invitation describing the approach and introducing the ground rules. They also receive a telephone call from one of the two facilitators in which they can express any hopes or concerns they have about the dialogue. These pre-meeting calls give facilitators an opportunity to make personal contact with participants, to answer any questions that arise, and to identify and potentially screen out people who are uncertain about their willingness or ability to engage in a dialogue at that time. The intention during this phase, and in the opening phases of the dialogue, is to proactively prevent polarized conversation and to prepare participants for a truly new conversation. When the dialogue participants understand the approach and are prepared to have a respectful conversation, the facilitators can take more of a back seat role during the dialogue.

The three-and-a-half hour meeting begins with dinner, during which participants are asked not to reveal where they stand on the issue they are on, but simply to meet others with whom they will share the evening. This is a time when people get to know each other on a personal level, share a meal, and often find themselves trying to guess who is on which side.

Participants then sit in assigned seats in a circle, with people of different views sitting next to each other and the facilitators sitting side by side. The facilitators introduce the process and review the three basic ground rules, asking the participants for suggestions and agreements about them. The first ground rule requires confidentiality and anonymity; the second ground rule, called the pass option, gives participants the right to pass if they are not ready or willing to answer a question at that point in the dialogue; and the third ground rule ensures respectful communication in which participants are asked to listen attentively while actively trying to understand, let others finish speaking, be aware of "air time," and avoid using disrespectful language.

In the first part of the dialogue, each participant is asked to respond to three questions, in three separate "go-arounds," with clear time limits. Each go-around is preceded by a moment of silence during which participants can collect their thoughts so that they can fully listen to others when the speaking begins. Note the way in which questions are framed so that participants are encouraged to use first-person speech and to talk about themselves at this point, rather than about some objective view of the issue at hand.

- What events or other personal life experiences may have shaped your current views and feelings about abortion? Could you tell us something about one or two of these events or experiences?

- Speaking as an individual, what is at the heart of the matter for *you*?

- Do *you* experience any mixed feelings, value conflicts, uncertainties, or other dilemmas within *your* overall perspective on this issue? (italics added) (Public Conversation Project, forthcoming)

The second part of the session is a time to ask questions of each other. Participants are encouraged to seek clarification if they do not understand another participant and to ask questions arising from genuine curiosity. They are explicitly asked to avoid rhetorical and accusatory questions. The evening concludes with participants reflecting on what has transpired and on the role they each have played in making the dialogue go as it has. The dialogue ends with no intent to put a neat bow on the process, to come to any resolution, or to make proposals for action at that point. They are informed about an ongoing group for "graduates" of the introductory dialogues—the New Ground Network—which meets monthly.

The one-session model described here was developed by PCP during its first two years (1990–1992). Since then, PCP has tested its general approach with people divided over other issues such as population and women's health, the environment, sexual orientation, and social class differences (Chasin and others, 1996). The experiences of people in PCP's sessions show that within the context of safety and respect, a shift can occur "from one of opposition to one of interest—and sometimes to one of compassion and even empathic connection" (Becker and others, 1995, p. 146).

The first-person speech of PCP's model is helpful in diffusing the usual way we tend to choose sides. It discourages the tendency to begin conversation by appealing to the support of experts, scholars, and authors in order to bolster a position and to silence or belittle the opposition with seemingly irrefutable evidence. Instead, participants are asked to talk about their stance from a personal perspective. Participants come as people, not debaters, representatives, or defenders of a position.

The PCP approach to designing the opening phases of an introductory dialogue establishes a starting place for relationships to emerge across the lines of division. It creates a context for honesty, for listening and being heard, and for a way of personally owning an issue as people speak of their individual points of conflict and confusion with the issue. This approach gets participants talking and listening as individuals with names and feelings, not as stereotypes. It allows participants to hear the genuine passion and motivation that compels people on the other side. Such a gathering makes it possible to see and hear each other as sisters and brothers again. It also invites participants to explore consciously, perhaps for the first time, why the issue is important to them. This discovery alone can make the dialogue worthwhile.

The PCP approach to the opening phases of dialogue strongly emphasizes personal speaking and does not provide a forum for in-depth dialogue about the details of the issue being discussed, which are often important to participants, such as the latest medical findings on homosexuality as a pre-birth characteristic or the biblical position on abortion. However, participants may speak about the meaning they ascribe to medical or biblical information as individuals and from their personal experiences. Discussions on specific aspects of the abortion controversy can and do take place in PCP's New Ground Network, where participants not only have more time together but also are less vulnerable to getting stuck in old battles because they have developed trusting relationships, a genuine interest in understanding each other, and a shared commitment to new ways of interacting.

The success of PCP's approach depends to a great degree on the facilitators' effectiveness. Facilitators must keep the tone and timing of the evening moving at a healthy pace without dictating too much of the process. They must also be prepared to enforce the ground rules and help participants reframe rhetorical questions to express their curiosity. Finally, the choice of the facilitators will affect the willingness of the conflicted sides to agree to participate in the process. If some are concerned that the facilitators favor one side over the other, the dialogue is likely to be impaired.

PCP's approach initiates a dialogue. It emphasizes creating a new conversation and shifting current relationships. The hope is that participants will discover enough energy and motivation to forge the next steps, which may include collaborative action or continued participation in facilitated conversations. Sometimes the impacts of these dialogues are more informal and subtle, as when, in their everyday lives, participants find themselves interested in understanding a difference of opinion or testing out a derogatory assumption they are making about another person by asking that person a genuinely respectful question.

Depth

> We will explore the complexity of needs, interests, feelings, and convictions that underlie the various positions on the issue. We will search for the secondary, interconnected issues and assumptions behind the presenting issue. We will be cautious of quick, easy solutions that appear to heal instantly or to convert others to our side, but merely mask the point of disagreement.

Entering the depths of an issue can be a frightening proposition. Just as entering the depths of a cave or the ocean is dangerous but invigorating, so too is plumbing the depths of an issue. As a participant in theological dialogues put it, "Because I trust in God, I can risk attending to the uncharted places of an issue, that is, the grey areas in my thinking. In fact, the grey areas may be the largest areas of common ground for all of us, no matter what side of an issue we're on. We're all human. There's always more to God than we can conceive or understand. The exciting thing is that going into the depths of an issue will lead us to the edge of our learning, to that place where the Spirit is inviting us."

Mathewes-Green found that exploring the depths of the abortion issue helped her clarify the questions and hone a direction for the next phase of her work on the issue. "The abortion issue has become something like a football game where yards gained by one side are by necessity yards lost by the other, and neither side is ever going to be willing to give up the fight. This polarization make it less likely that we can arrive at a resolution; and without resolution, consensus, and peace on this issue, there will be no lasting protection for the unborn. . . . A *deeper agreement* must be reached. . . . " (italics added) (1998).

One way to deepen the dialogue is through programs such as the Common Ground Network for Life and Choice (CGN) (see Chapter Three). By beginning with common concern and conviction, CGN helps groups in dispute work together out of a place of unity, and evaluate their places of difference from a common point of reference.

Key to this model is the process of "rehumanizing" the people on the other side of the issue by listening and speaking with care. This process requires the development of *connective thinking* skills. Connective thinking assumes that every participant has some unique knowledge and understanding of the truth that can be connected to the group's collective knowledge in order to link together the best wisdom of each participant. As one participant in a CGN dialogue observed, "Instead of looking at the other as an antagonist and feeling the need to stake out one's turf, there is an emphasis on relationships, on unity, on creating a way of welcoming one another rather than fighting one another."

The CGN workshop is an all-day, six- or seven-hour event, including lunch. In a large-group setting, participants introduce themselves, explain why they chose to attend, and state where they stand on the issue (for example, pro-choice or pro-life participant, or facilitator). The assembly is then broken into small groups with a facilitator to discuss personal experiences that brought them to their current stance on the issue in dispute.

Participants then rate twenty-five statements of beliefs on the disputed subject from 1 to 5, where 1 indicates strong agreement and 5 indicates strong disagreement. They are then asked to rate the statements a second time as they think people on the other side of the issue would respond. These answers are tabulated to reveal points of similarity, difference, and misperception. In small groups, participants discuss how they have experienced being misunderstood and stereotyped and what they think can come out of discovering common ground. According to CGN, this conversation often results in a call for further united activities on behalf of the common concern or for further gatherings to delve deeper into the dialogue.

Senge offers a simple exercise called "the Wall," which is a resource for helping a dialogue group move deeper into an issue. Participants work together to identify all the variables, related issues, and questions that come from the presenting issue. Each variable is written on a sheet of paper. Participants then use a wall and tape to sort and arrange the variables into natural groupings and to consider if any larger issues link together the grouped issues. This exercise is also a reminder that, given the issue's complexity, no single position can claim to be the final, definitive answer that solves all of the presenting issues once and for all.

Patience

Because we recognize that good dialogue is always a sustained conversation, we will stay with the process and not avoid or abandon the dialogue.

Dialogue develops through conversation with adversaries in which personal relationships are established, a new language is learned, feelings and underlying issues are explored, and a commitment is made to join in growing through the interaction. All of this requires a major investment of time.

Most religious leaders and active laypeople report that the main reason they are not involved in formal dialogue is because they lack the time. They have counted the costs in terms of time and have found it to be too expensive. A survey of pastors in one city revealed that lack of time was the major limitation on dialogue participation by everyone questioned. "There is simply a limit to what I can pour myself into," lamented one pastor. "It's not worth my time," said the pastor of a large church. "There's nothing to be gained from it. I even quit having our denominational paper sent to our members. All it does is stir people up about things I can't do anything about."

A pastor on the Right said, "My focus has to be on my local church and the issues inside it. I'm more focused on individual and family issues than on larger societal issues. I may care about the abortion issue, but rather than join a protest march I'd rather counsel members who do, or help the church be involved in the Crisis Center." A Left pastor said, "It takes too much time, yields little or no progress, and is most often antagonistic. Frankly, it takes too much time and energy to be nice."

If this is the sentiment of clergy who are engaged in the mission of the church on a full-time basis, one can only imagine the difficulty for laypeople to make the time commitment required for formal dialogue. If dialogue is another activity to be added to the church's overfilled schedules, it will soon be forsaken. To overcome the time crunch, dialogue must be viewed as a way to achieve some of the goals already set for a church, such as growing in trust of God, deepening Christian education, engaging in ecumenical conversation, and embodying the healing and hope of God's reconciling love.

Still, there's no denying that dialogue takes time and patience. Effective dialogue resists the temptation to turn the interaction into a "task" that must be completed, cataloged, and filed. Dialogue, like the work of the Spirit, cannot be assigned a schedule. It is an ongoing experience, a process of "mindfulness," as some dialogue leaders describe it, with no obvious starting or ending place. In fact, dialogue begins before adversaries ever agree to talk, and they continue in the minds of the participants long after talks have ended. One leader described a dialogue between two schools of thought within a national social work agency that began at an annual meeting, continued the next year, skipped a year, and came to resolution in the following year.

Dialogue is an exciting venture for the church. Using the Ten Guidelines for Dialogue will deepen any conversation and open new vistas in ongoing conflicts. The Ten Guidelines provide tools to unearth the common ground between us and our adversaries, and to establish a foundation on which new possibilities for building together can emerge—in communities, schools, industry, and nations.

One place where dialogue finds a particular challenge, unfortunately, is among Christians. Christians are told repeatedly in the Bible that we are one in Christ. But we are also programmed through years of benevolent training to remain on one side or the other of an elusive, invisible line that sends the church into two vague but real directions. Can and should Christians erase this line? Or are there ways to cope with the many, varied views within the church and at the same time live out the unity described and commanded by Jesus?

5

Understanding Why Christians Fight

I n Austin, Texas, as in many cities across the country, Christian churches participate in one of two different citywide marches: the March for Jesus, an interdenominational praise march, or the CROP Walk, also an interdenominational march used as a fund-raiser for church hunger-relief agencies. The first march celebrates God's dominion in the world and proclaims the need for our country to return to the biblical God. The second march extols the virtue of Christian advocacy on behalf of those excluded from the bounty of God's world.

The two marches take place at different times in the year. The entire Christian community is invited to participate in both events, but only a few churches participate in both marches. "Orthodox," or Right, churches from virtually every denomination participate in the March for Jesus. "Progressive," or Left, churches from these same denominations can be found marching in the CROP Walk.

What's going on here? We know that March for Jesus churches care about feeding the hungry. And we know that CROP Walk churches love God and want to see our nation return to a morality centered in God. So what is it that divides us? Why don't we march together? Because an invisible line separates us into CROP Walk churches and March for Jesus churches.

This chapter explores the elusive, invisible line that delineates the progressives from the orthodox, or Left from Right. Is this a chasm that can be bridged? Is it possible for groups to dialogue meaningfully across this line, or are we forever doomed to shout at one another from across an unbridgeable chasm? Do we even have a choice concerning which side of the line we are on, or is our place on the line determined by outside forces?

Taking Sides

Setting a line of demarcation between the two sides is a complex, subjective task. It can be made easy, of course, by reducing the issue to simply noting how we take sides on issues that divide us. These concerns can include general issues of public debate, such as abortion, capital punishment, prayer in public schools, school vouchers, homosexuality, environmental issues, and the role of government in legislating moral issues. Within the church we are also divided by specifically church-related concerns, such as the terms we use to describe the Bible, how we interpret the Bible, the use of inclusive language, the role of women in church, worship styles, or more far-reaching theological questions such as, "What about the heathen?"

Groups cluster around similar positions on most of these issues. Enough exceptions exist within these groups, however, to make one cautious about assuming that this is an adequate way to choose sides. For example, a Pentecostal minister described his experience of attending a meeting sponsored by the National Council of Churches, clearly an organization on the other side of the culture war from him. A United Methodist clergywoman approached him and said, "We're glad to have you here. And yet, I must admit that the presence of a Pentecostal raises new concerns and puts an issue on the back burner that is important for me; namely, feminism. We've worked hard to make women's issues a priority. Now I guess we'll be forced to talk about other things." The Pentecostal minister felt stereotyped and dismissed. "She didn't know it," he later reflected, "but I might have been her ally. After all, my grandmother was a Pentecostal pastor!"

It is instructive to note that the "side" we are on is not based on the particular answer we give to a specific question. For example, on the question of the appropriateness of mandated prayer in public schools, a Baptist and an atheist may agree, despite the fact that they may approach the issue from opposite sides of the Faith Divide. The same may be true of the pacifist and the political conservative on the question of military intervention in Bosnia, or the Jew and the fundamentalist Christian on how the United States should relate to Israel.

A second, popular method of choosing sides within the church is to look at different understandings of the Bible. Those who believe the Bible is "literally true" are considered conservative; those who allow for ambiguity and context when reading the Bible are considered liberal. As with the first method of choosing sides, this pattern has too many exceptions to be trusted without question. "Literalists" are rarely literal in their reading of the Bible, and "liberals" become literalists when reading a passage about justice or feeding the hungry.

A third way we take sides is by uniting against an identified enemy. Often our caricatures of the enemy are overstated for clarity and in order to win the majority to our side. The orthodox Right can depict its enemy as "godlessness," whether in political systems such as communism, or ideological systems such as secular humanism. For example, James Dobson, a popular conservative leader, depicts his adversaries as those who have moved from "God is . . ." to "God isn't, . . . where the only rule is what seems right" (1995, p. 28). The progressive Left, on the other hand, may try to describe its enemy in terms of a selfishness that excludes others—monetarily, religiously, or socially. As one pastor put it, "Our country is not threatened by the New Age Movement or by secularism as much as it is by fundamentalists. It is the one thing that is clearly in opposition to the gospel." This method of choosing sides is also flawed; for example, liberal Catholics and fundamentalist Protestants find themselves chagrined as they team together to fight for passage of a school voucher program. Politics makes strange bedfellows.

Simple, quick attempts to draw a clear line of demarcation between "us" and "them" fall short. The division is complex and multifaceted, as Wuthnow notes in his analysis of the culture war, *The Struggle for America's Soul* (1989). Wuthnow integrates the many societal factors, especially within the last quarter century, that combine with various theological disagreements in the church to give rise to the present "two-party" system within both religion and society as a whole. He cites such factors as the rise in educational levels, memories of the Holocaust, regional migration and resulting contact with diverse groups, interreligious marriage, and the civil rights movement as trends that contributed to a sense of tolerance, or progressivism, among many in our culture.

Jack Rogers offers another theory. He contends that the breakdown of a fairly universally-held American world view occurred in the mid-nineteenth century. Two factors caused this breakdown: the approaching Civil War and the North's and South's different readings of what the Bible says about slavery, and the emergence of Darwin's theory of evolution (Rogers, 1995, p. 15).

In either case, the resulting climate meant that the values of old were questioned and modified by a new generation. Those who still revered the traditional values naturally objected. Sides formed and conflict ensued. Conservatives, or the orthodox, championed the traditional values that shaped our moral standards, whereas liberals, or progressives, focused on mutual respect and actions that could effect positive change in the world.

The acceptability of either analysis depends on where one stands in relation to it. Typically, these characterizations of two discernible sides are too broad and negative to be accepted by the sides being described. Characterizations compete. What one side describes as "tolerant," the other side views as "permissive." One side's "conviction" looks "narrow-minded" to the other side. Talk of "love and grace" is a sign of virtue for one side, but may indicate sloppy, slippery theology to the other side.

Other questions arise: How much choice do we have in choosing our side in the conflicts within the church? Are we predisposed to one side or the other by virtue of our birth and surroundings, much as we acquire our accents or mannerisms? There is little doubt that many or most of our deeply held convictions and attitudes are handed down to us from our homes and other spheres of influence from which we have emerged. How much can be attributed to these spheres, and how much of our temperaments and tendencies toward one side or the other of a divisive issue are a function of the personalities we have at birth? And can any amount of education or moral persuasion entice us to switch sides at a level deeper than simply altering our behavior patterns? Scholars like Milton Rokeach explore this question in such complex works as his *Beliefs, Attitudes, and Values* (1968). This is the old nature versus nurture question all over again.

A sizable group stakes a claim in the "center," attempting to balance themselves in the very middle of, or at times *above*, the invisible line. This is not surprising, since most dialogue participants would like to be known as part of *the* centrist, conciliatory group. Being in the center seems to imply reasonableness, moderation, and civility. But the competition for the center does not deny the reality of a basic division within the church any more than Switzerland's neutrality during World War II meant there was no war being fought in the 1940s. Being in the center simply means some Christians hope to remain noncommittal by declaring themselves in the middle. Maybe they can, but at what price?

There is no denying the spectrum of positions on either side of an invisible line in the church. We are like snowflakes, no two alike. Nor can we deny the beauty of a truly courageous and conciliatory Christian center where civility and conviction are joined. The center plays a valuable role in bringing the church's conflicted sides together. Nonetheless, recognizing the reality of two broadly discernible sides separated by an invisible line of demarcation is a helpful and necessary step for beginning the work of dialogue.

If, as Wuthnow suggests, the reasons we find ourselves on one side or the other of the invisible line are complex and multifaceted, then none of us can retrace the steps or untangle the factors that led us to the conclusions we now hold on issues that divide the church. The road back to our beginnings is too winding, with too many choices made from motives and influences long forgotten or never known. But at some point we find ourselves on one side or the other of an invisible line that defines and divides us.

Left and Right of What?

The "invisible line" is faith's version of the Continental Divide, that imperceptible north-south line running through the Rocky Mountains of North America where waters from the top of the mountains divide, flowing either west to the Pacific or east to the Atlantic. At the line of the Faith Divide is a question, the same question Pontius Pilate asked Jesus long ago: "What is truth?" (John 18:38).

"What is truth?" takes many different forms: "What is good?" "Who is saved?" "Who or what determines the rules by which we live?" "What does God want?" "What is God doing?" "Where is the world headed?" "Can our understanding of truth ever be accurate?" Typically, the truth question is even more specific: Is a particular value or action considered good? Is this or that particular group saved? Does a certain behavior conform to the rules by which I think the world should live? Behind all of these questions is a desire to tap into what is right and true.

Most Christians are only occasionally confronted outright with the truth question as a theological or philosophical problem, and when we are, most of us are bored, except for a few theorists. Instead, we are confronted by the more practical, less abstract forms of the question, such as questions about prayer in school or whether to vote for a political candidate based on his or her view of abortion. Underlying all of these questions, however, is the bare, raw question Pilate asked of Jesus: "What is truth?"

Social psychologist Milton Rokeach's *The Open and Closed Mind* offers a visual depiction of the truth question. Rokeach contends, "It is not so much *what* you believe that counts, but *how* you believe" (1960, p. 6). Like the proposed faith divide, Rokeach suggests that an important distinction in looking at varieties of belief systems is whether people, conservative or liberal, hold their beliefs, in a structure that is "closed," that is, insisting that others agree or conform to their particular beliefs, or whether the structure is "open" to exploring other possibilities or insights in addition to their own.

Figure 5.1, a simplification of Rokeach's thoughts, suggests that the spectrum of beliefs has two dimensions: the content of beliefs and how we relate to each other's beliefs. Each U.S. church denomination could be generally located in relation to another denomination on a point on the horizontal, liberal-conservative axis, which represents the content of its beliefs. Each denomination can also be located on Rokeach's vertical, open-closed axis, which represents

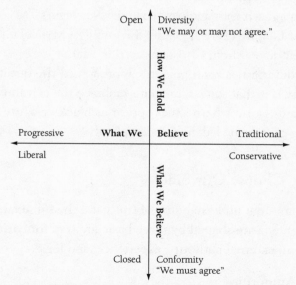

Figure 5.1. Content of One's Beliefs Intersecting with How One Relates to Others' Beliefs.

From Rokeach, Milton. *The Open and Closed Mind*. New York: Basic Books, 1960.

how one relates to other believers and their understanding of truth. Both lines impact our view of truth.

The approaches each of us take to the church's divisive questions, approaches that locate us on one side or the other of the Faith Divide, finally come down to our basic convictions about truth and to the enormous issues that philosophers place under the heading of epistemology. The questions raised in this field of study include, How do we know what we know? Is truth knowable by humans to the degree that we can say that *all* people should live by the moral values that we know to be true? Or is truth something that even Christians hold with human limitations, and on which we can live by faith alone? Is one's understanding of truth exclusive or inclusive? Is it static or dynamic? Is one's understanding and application of truth secure and fixed? Or is it open to correction and the possibility of receiving deeper, more profound insights into the nature of the gospel? Here is the essence of Rokeach's two-dimensional continuum and the invisible line of the Faith Divide. (For an example of how Christians from the Right approach epistemology, see Leslie Newbigin's *The Gospel in a Pluralistic Culture* (1989); Daniel Taylor's *The Myth of Certainty* (1992) offers a view from Christians on the Left).

What determines each person's approach to the question of truth? Why is it that some Christians embrace the certainty of an unambiguous world where issues appear as black or white, while others find every issue laden with complexity?

How We Choose Our Side

As Christians, our understanding of truth and the subsequent values we embrace are shaped by three basic areas of formation and information: external authority, experience, and logic.

External Authorities

External authorities, or derived beliefs, for Christians include the Bible, church tradition—its history, customs, precedents, and convictions—and current church leaders, namely, its pastors and teachers. These various forms of authority all hold sway for Christians but are invariably interrelated to each other in their interpretation and application. One source, usually the Bible, is more authoritative than the others, but *all* have authority in most Christians' lives.

The Bible, tradition, and leaders are *external* sources of authority because all three function as authority from outside of us and can do so only if and when we assign or concede authority to them. What we receive from these authorities varies depends on what level of authority is granted: Do they have authority only to raise the question, or also to give the answer? Authority to shape us, or to tell us? To set the parameters, or to give the details?

The degree of authority we grant these external sources falls somewhere on a spectrum ranging from absolute authority to relative authority. The extreme absolutist grants one or all of these authorities the absolute right to determine for him or her the value of a view or moral position. The extreme relativist would deny these authorities any value beyond their historical or sectarian significance. Between these two extremes lies a spectrum containing an infinite number of degrees of authority.

At some point, maturing Christians ask themselves, How did I decide the degree of authority I have granted to each of these sources? And is my decision valid? This can be a time of affirmation, re-prioritizing, or reconfiguring one's beliefs.

Personal Experience

The second source of information in our understanding of truth is *personal experience*. Unlike external authorities, experience is chiefly an internal source of authority. It is our own personal history that shapes both how we view the world and the values we hold.

For example, a person raised in the home of an abusive alcoholic might have a different understanding of and sensitivity to the issues surrounding the use of alcohol than someone who does not share this experience. Similarly, survivors of the Great Depression often have a different ethic about work and money than people born in later years. The child of a Christian Scientist home is shaped, positively or negatively, to embody the values espoused in that household. Some accept the beliefs handed down to them; others reject these beliefs; none are unaffected by the beliefs and assumptions that surround us in the world in which we are raised. That is to say, we do not form our personal experiences on our own. We are social creatures, shaped by the milieu of our formative years. Our experiences throughout life, good and bad, subtly shape our responses to every new value question we consider.

One's personal experience of God (and the way that experience is valued and interpreted by significant others) may also significantly shape how open or closed one is on the question of truth. Is God experienced more as the One bringing shape and order to chaos, much like the God of Genesis 1? Or is God experienced as the liberator of those in bondage, more like the Yahweh of Exodus? For some, truth resides primarily in the order and rules of God that are eternal and true. For others, truth is experienced primarily in the grace and freedom that comes with an encounter with God. Although these images should not be mutually exclusive, it is easy to see how one's experience of God and the dominant image of the Divine in scripture to which a person is drawn will give primal direction to one's position in the various points of conflict among Christians.

Personality and temperament also affect how we deal with the truth question. Some people appear to be born with a strong need for security, stability, rules, and rhythm. Others rebel against these aspects of life, preferring the exuberance of risk, discovery, and freedom. These traits inform the way we experience life and shape how we respond to the question of truth.

Logic

Logic, the third factor in our approach to truth, can be both an external authority, such as the logic of philosophy or the natural sciences, and an internal authority, by way of personal reasoning. For example, on the abortion question, we receive information from science about when human life begins. The logic from this external authority intersects with our personal reasoning, then is assimilated with other facts and opinions at our disposal, along with our own personal intuition and convictions. Like the previous authority-shaper, experience, logic is a fluid and subjective process. One person's logic is another person's confusion.

These three sources—external authorities, experience, and logic—combine in countless ways to make us who we are. They shape us, and of course, we also shape them. (And even these sources of authority are shaped by the present pervasive influence of the culture around us, which is involved in a culture war.) The result is an infinite number of points on the spectrum of understanding truth, each with its own nuance and rationale that is shaped by, and in turn shapes, how we use these sources of truth. But in the end, when we finally work our way down to the basic questions, these countless and unique positions fall either to the Left or the Right of the Faith Divide on the most basic question of all—the question of truth: Is life based on a truth that is singular or plural, fixed or fluid, accessible or remote?

Winds of War

Just as the Continental Divide sends waters in different directions, so too our approach to truth sends Christians in essentially two different directions from the Faith Divide: some to the left and some to the right. "Right" and "Left" are terms we sometimes employ to denote the distinct direction of movement between those we might call absolutist, orthodox, or closed (Right) for their emphasis on truth as clear, set, and universal; and those we might call pluralist, progressive, or open (Left) for their belief in more than one angle to truth and its applications.

There is a division, a split. The split, the Faith Divide, is not always extreme. Not all of the westward-flowing water makes it all the way to the Pacific, nor does all the eastward-flowing water reach the Atlantic. Sometimes the split is a thin, imperceptible line. On many questions of moral value the Left and Right of today's Christian conflicts generally agree. We may move in different directions, but we are all water, and all water comes from Above, and both the Atlantic and Pacific remain connected to the same continent.

But at the line of the Divide, on the underlying question of the nature of truth, a discernible flow exists to the left and right. And when the two sides arrive at conclusions that appear to be mutually exclusive, as is the case with many of today's highly visible moral issues, we no longer feel connected to those on the other side. To the contrary, we feel alienated from each other. The very presence of other Christians coming at an issue from a vastly different direction produces a sense of anxiety which, in turn, causes a subsequent mobilizing of resources. Inevitably, deeply-held convictions result in actions, reactions, and if the pattern persists, war.

That Christians differ on issues is hardly a new phenomenon, as the account of the early church throughout the book of Acts reminds us. What is noteworthy, and problematic, is the role we assign these differences. Jack Rogers observes that "conflict occurs when people—Christian people—make their theological elaborations or ideological applications or experiential colorings the ultimate rather than the ultimate religious world view itself. In Christian terms, conflict occurs when we put anything at the center except our commitment to God revealed in Jesus Christ" (1995, p. xvii).

Shall We Capitalize on Our Conflicts?

The answer to this rather philosophical question, "What is truth?" is never simply a disembodied theory, but becomes incarnate in our institutions and political systems. It is expressed in our various churches and clubs, our causes and concerns. Our ideas take on flesh. And flesh begets flesh. In the divided context of our conflict within the church, any incarnation of a view of truth leads to the birth of a second, competing incarnation. For example, the rise of the Christian Coalition was the occasion for the birth of its counterpart, the Interfaith Alliance. The Moral Majority was matched by People for the American Way. Operation Rescue was matched by the National Abortion Rights Action League. Within denominations, a conservative splinter group is countered by the creation of a liberal group.

These enormous alliances form to espouse the virtue of one side of the competing visions of truth. It is big business, typically bigger and noisier around election time. The result is a highly-financed publicity battle between the competing views of truth—all in an effort to win the support and minds of undecided people across the country. These incarnations of ideas mobilize and equip their constituents. Newspapers, mailing lists, speakers, bureaus, rallies, and web pages emerge to get out the word, and they are always met with counterparts on the other side. They solidify the polarization and complicate the possibility for hopeful dialogue. A kind of Christian culture war is waged by these institutions, both as an ideological concern and as a way to justify their continued existence. The bottom line is that it is in the best interest of these institutions to see the culture war continue, even grow. Thus, they keep the rhetoric hot and the polarization fixed.

At their extremes, neither the Left nor the Right are worthy candidates for dialogue. They cannot talk because they have nothing to talk about. Both have closed systems of thought. Extremists on the Right are convinced that they know the truth. Their moral values are undeniable and non-negotiable. Truth has taken up residence in their faith perspective. Truth is objective. All other perspectives are subjective or wrong, and it is the responsibility of those on the Right to correct others, rather than encounter them and learn of and from them.

The Left extremists are also convinced they know the truth. Their truth is relativism. Taken to its extreme this position results in "an undiscriminating twilight in which 'all cats are gray,' all perspectives equally viable, and as a result equally uncompelling" (Eck, 1993, p. 193). Engaging in dialogue with extreme relativists is like trying to stand in quicksand: there is nothing firm to stand on. If everything is "absolutely relative" (an oxymoron, of course), what is left to say? Like their counterparts on the Right, extremists on the Left are equally adamant that their positions are objectively true and non-negotiable.

When we consider dialogue, the temptation always exists to dismiss our adversaries as extremists. This tactic allows us to avoid our enemies by not taking them seriously. But to yield to this temptation is to miss an encounter that could be one of great growth and grace. Rather than avoid each other, we need to ask ourselves, What are the implications of the church staying solely on the left or right of the faith divide? Can we do anything with our basic differences of view other than simply perpetuate the destruction and demoralization of the culture war? Are we doomed to fight an endless (and meaningless) theological tug-of-war, or can we reframe the dilemma in a way that recognizes the various positions in a conflict as distinct and yet valuable? Do we miss something if we avoid dialogue, something to be learned or reclaimed if the church were free to move back and forth between the left or right?

Chapter Six provides a unique model for framing our differences in a way that moves us from either-or thinking to both-and thinking. It sees issues such as the conflicts within the Christian church as "polarities to manage rather than problems to solve" (Johnson, 1992).

6

Turning Our Differences
into Sources of Growth

If there is a Faith Divide that moves Christians away from each other, is there any way to minimize or even redeem this invisible, divisive line? Can we let it be a line of demarcation without allowing it to become a chasm between Christians? Is it even possible for our differences to become an asset instead of a liability?

My contention is that dialogue provides a framework for Christians in conflict to begin relating to one another and transforming our divisions into sources of growth. Dialogue values the views of all participants and claims that real depth and growth can occur only when we invite our adversaries to help us see reality from their point of view. This assumes that our assumptions about a clear-cut line between us and them, good and bad, right and wrong are temporarily suspended in dialogue so that we can learn from a vantage point that is not our own.

This is no small task. We've all been trained to think that when we have a right answer, anyone who disagrees with our view is wrong. If disagreements are "bad," then it would be inappropriate to welcome a different view. In contrast, dialogue risks exploring our differences in order to determine whether they can be used as a tool for growth. Dialogue asks us if what appears at the outset of a conflict to be bad or wrong may be simply a different but valid view of reality.

A valuable tool to aid dialogue in transforming the conflict between opposing positions is Barry Johnson's Polarity Management™

model. Johnson, a consultant working with business and religious bodies, contends that many large, complex problems are actually "polarities to manage, not problems to solve." By polarities, Johnson means that the two sides of an issue that appear opposite and in conflict with each other are two parts of the same whole. Although it appears the poles are out to destroy each other, in fact they work together. "In order to gain and maintain the benefits of one pole, you must also pursue the benefits of the other" (1992, p. 23). The poles are interdependent; if one side of an argument is not counterbalanced by the other side, its effectiveness is diminished. This will be more apparent as we explore Polarity Management.

Interdependency is one of the qualities that distinguish polarities to manage from problems to solve. The other quality is that conflict is an ongoing concern, rather than a temporary problem.

Using these criteria, a strong case can be made that the Left-Right traditionalist-progressive conflict within the Christian church qualifies as a polarity to manage rather than a problem to solve. Certainly, the conflict in which we are embroiled today is nothing new; it has been a part of the American Christian story throughout this century. If, as some posit, the conflict between traditionalists and progressives can be understood as a basic tension between law and grace, then we recognize that this polarity dominated the letters of Paul to the early church.

The Flow of Polarities

Johnson uses the activity of breathing to illustrate the polarity management process. Inhaling is a benefit to the body, bringing it needed oxygen. But inhaling alone is inadequate. Eventually exhaling is necessary to rid the body of carbon dioxide. The "competing" activities of inhaling and exhaling are not solved by either-or thinking, for they are not problems to be solved, but polarities to be managed. A flow, an infinity loop, exists between the two polarities that moves the body from one action to the other. In order to maintain balance, the body must willingly flow from inhalation to exhalation and back again. The two actions are interdependent. (See Figure 6.1.)

In order to supplement either-or thinking with both-and thinking, polarity management discourages referring to the strengths of a polarity as a "solution," for to do so is to set it up to be called a "mistake" later. Rather, this model recognizes that every polarity has an "upside (+)" as well as a "downside (–)" and that to linger too long in a particular polarity's "upside" will inevitably bring about some of the "downside" to that polarity (1992).

The insights of Polarity Management offer new hope for conflicts among Christians by providing a framework that could alter the way we approach our present impasses. Could the issue underlying the split between liberal-conservative, open-closed, traditionalist-progressive, Left-Right be framed as a polarity to be managed instead of a problem to be solved through one side winning over the other? Can we acknowledge that both sides of the Divide have an upside as well as a downside? Could the many divisions among Christians today be the result of the kind of either-or problem solving that

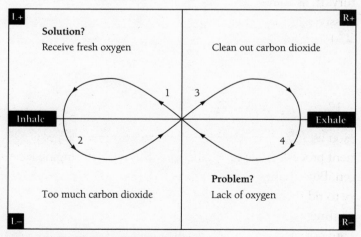

Figure 6.1. The Balance of Breathing.
Reprinted from *Polarity Management*, Barry Johnson, 1992. Reprinted by permission of the publisher, HRD Press, Amherst, MA.

produces some temporary winners but ultimately yields only losers, and that never creates the sense of unity and wholeness that Polarity Management contends is possible?

Building a Theological Left-Right Polarity Map

If the conflict within the Christian church can be largely understood in terms of the split between the Left and the Right, or progressives and traditionalists, then our map will look like Figure 6.2.

One way to begin filling in a polarity map is to list the downside of one of the polarities by reciting the concerns and fears cited by critics on the other side. It doesn't matter which pole is filled in first. Eventually the process is applied to the up and downsides of both polarities.

Let's begin with the downside to the progressive Christian perspective. The following concerns are frequently cited (see Figure 6.3):

- Progressives are so wishy-washy and liberal in their convictions that virtually any belief or action can be acceptable.

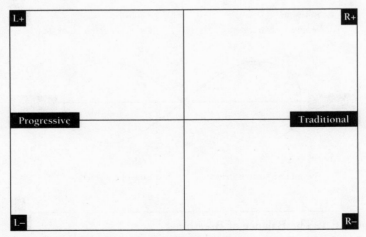

Figure 6.2. Split Within Polarized Church.
Reprinted from *Polarity Management*, Barry Johnson, 1992. Reprinted by permission of the publisher, HRD Press, Amherst, MA.

- Progressives view history and tradition as relics of the past that have no claim on the decisions and values of today.

- Winning people to the Lord becomes secondary or even meaningless compared to progressives' call to do justice.

- Progressives want to turn our government into a secular, Godless state.

- Progressives disregard the Bible.

- Progressives end up with no deep relationship with God.

The response or reaction to the downside of the progressive pole (L–) becomes the upside of the opposite, or traditionalist pole (R+). When asked to list the ways this pole counteracts the deficiencies of the L-pole, we hear the following strengths (see Figure 6.4):

- Evangelical churches make a clear and unambiguous presentation of rules for Christian living.

- Traditionalists recognize that the tradition of the church serves as a precedent for today.

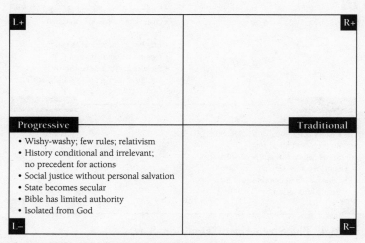

Figure 6.3. The Weaknesses of Progressives.
Reprinted from *Polarity Management*, Barry Johnson, 1992. Reprinted by permission of the publisher, HRD Press, Amherst, MA.

- Traditionalists emphasize winning people to Christ and having their lives changed.

- Traditionalists have a reverence for both God and country.

- The Bible is firmly held to as the unambiguous author-ity for life's answers.

- Traditionalists understand themselves to have a unique relationship with God through Jesus.

Johnson notes that a movement to push from one pole to the other is caused by a group's displeasure with the "problem" of the present pole they perceive themselves to be in at the moment, as well as an attraction to the upside of the opposite pole as the "solution" to the problem. It is easy to see how many of us who love the church would want to move from the downside of the progressive pole to the upside of the traditionalist pole, and, as Simon Peter desired on the Mount of Transfiguration, to establish the church and dwell there forever. But just as Peter discovered about the Mount of Trans-figuration, the move from L– to R+, although positive, is not a

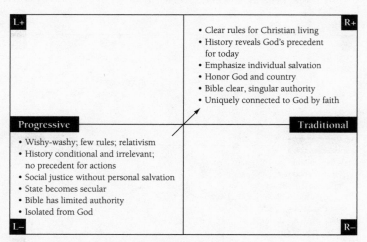

Figure 6.4. The Strengths of Traditionalists.
Reprinted from *Polarity Management*, Barry Johnson, 1992. Reprinted by per-mission of the publisher, HRD Press, Amherst, MA.

permanent home. The traditionalist side, when overemphasized or not balanced by the progressive side, has its downside too, as those on the Left are quick to point out. Eventually the good qualities of R+ slip to the traditionalist downside (R–) (see Fig. 6.5):

- Traditionalists want to legislate morality.

- Traditionalists think all issues of life have been resolved and carved into stone.

- Traditionalists don't care about the needy; they only care about winning people to Jesus.

- Traditionalists want to elect their religious leaders and turn the country into a fundamentalist Christian nation.

- Traditionalists think the Bible answers every question that is asked today.

- Traditionalists are out of touch with the rest of the world.

These "problems" are the natural results of viewing theological questions from only the traditionalist vantage point. The positions

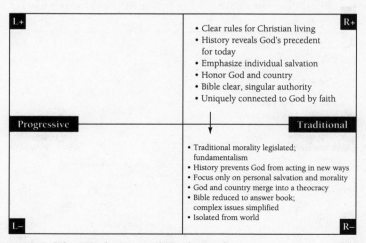

Figure 6.5. The Weaknesses of Traditionalists.
Reprinted from *Polarity Management*, Barry Johnson, 1992. Reprinted by permission of the publisher, HRD Press, Amherst, MA.

in R– are not necessarily where many advocates of R+ intended to be; in fact, traditionalists may be uncomfortable with the implications of R–. But what does one do? In the traditionalists' view, the R pole is far better than the L pole, because they value the upside of R and fear the downside of L.

Eventually, displeasure with the "problems" of the traditionalist pole and the desire for a "solution" to these problems moves believers who love the church to advocate for the upside of the Left pole. Note that the positions of L+ respond to the "problem" side of the Right. The movement to L+ is not a reaction to the upside of the Right, but rather a reaction to its vulnerable underbelly, its downside (see Figure 6.6):

- Progressive theology provides the freedom and flexibility to address the complexities of today's world.

- History reveals not only the patterns of God's involvement, but also recognizes the many unpredictable ways that God has acted.

- Liberal churches care for the forgotten children of God.

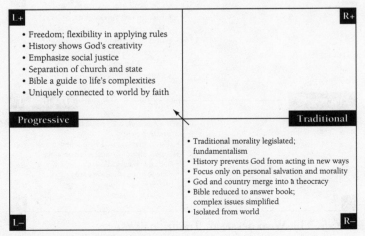

Figure 6.6. The Strengths of Progressives.
Reprinted from *Polarity Management*, Barry Johnson, 1992. Reprinted by permission of the publisher, HRD Press, Amherst, MA.

- Progressives have a healthy suspicion of the role of government in affairs of the church.

- Progressives take the Bible seriously, not literally.

- Their faith leads progressives to a deeper relationship with the needs of the world.

If the graph has been created accurately, the characteristics of L+, if not balanced with R+, will lead to L−, which is where we began. The completed diagram, shown in Figure 6.7, reveals one person's attempt to picture the progressive-traditional polarity, as well as the typical and necessary movement that continually occurs from one sector to another in the management of healthy polarities.

Those who advocate moving from the downside of one pole to the upside of the other pole are called "crusaders," and those who resist the movement from the upside of one pole to the downside of the other are called "tradition-bearers." Both groups play an important role: Crusaders have a vision and give energy to make improvements; tradition-bearers preserve what is good in the present pole and warn of the dangers of the downside of the opposite pole. In the

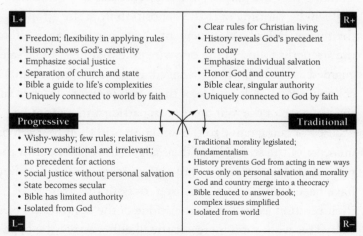

Figure 6.7. The Church's Flow Between Polarities.

Reprinted from *Polarity Management*, Barry Johnson, 1992. Reprinted by permission of the publisher, HRD Press, Amherst, MA.

heat of a battle, these two roles appear to fight each other; in the light of dialogue, it becomes clear that they form an odd, sometime unconscious alliance that works to achieve a higher purpose that transcends both poles.

Benefits of Polarity Management for Dialogue

Polarity Management benefits the work of dialogue in many ways, including the following:

1. Polarity Management helps dialogue avoid only either-or thinking, such as in, "Either the Bible is accepted as the sole, infallible authority for the church, or we will enter the slippery slope of relativism where nothing is true and nothing prohibited"; or, "We must keep the church open to the creative guidance of the Spirit, or we will fall prey to the legalism that confines us to the ways of the past"; or "Only my side of the invisible line is a faithful rendition of the gospel."

   Either-or thinking alone deludes dialogue participants into thinking that the purpose of the interaction is to solve the problem by winning over the opposition from the error of their ways. Polarity Management allows participants to affirm the strengths found in the opposite pole that need to be safeguarded as the polarity is managed. It also calls participants to acknowledge the downside of their own position. By spending time in each of the four quadrants, participants cannot be accused of being naive to the weaknesses in their position or unaware of the strengths of their adversaries' position. In the process of elaborating a polarity, participants know that they have been heard; opponents listen to both the strength of their position as well as their critique of the opposition's position. This realization increases the likelihood that the opposition, in turn, will listen and deepen the dialogue.

Polarity Management prevents one side from winning by supplementing either-or thinking with both-and thinking. As much as the Left and Right think they'd like to conquer their adversaries, without their adversaries they would end up at the downside of their poles.

Polarity Management encourages dialogue participants to distinguish between either-or thinking and both-and thinking. It recognizes that either-or thinking is appropriate for many problems that have only one right answer (Type 1 problems: Who was the first president? How much is 4 + 4?). In these cases, it would be inappropriate to entertain other "answers" to these questions as valid. On the other hand, either-or thinking is not appropriate for complex problems that are ongoing and that have two or more "right" answers that are interrelated (Type 2 problems: What is the proper balance between the needs of individuals and the needs of a community? How much stability should culture require in the face of the many changes of our day?).

Mistaking Type 2 problems for Type 1 problems is the source of the conflict impasses in which the church is currently mired.

2. Polarity Management invites dialogue participants to explore and name the range of strengths and weaknesses of the various positions in a conflict and to see the interrelationship between one side's weaknesses and the other side's strengths. Completing a polarity management graph allows participants to see a more complete picture of the conflict. This opportunity to see the whole picture allows participants to step back and recognize the part they play in both addressing the weakness of the other side, as well as creating strengths that counterbalance those weaknesses. At the same time, the opportunity to celebrate one's strengths provides a safe context in which to name and acknowledge the underbelly, or downside, to one's pole, and to recognize how concerns over those weaknesses could

cause others to move as crusaders to the upside of the opposite pole. This is a tremendous dialogue resource.

3. Polarity Management helps participants on the other side of an issue expand their reality. First, acknowledging the accuracy of their position (the + quadrant of their side, which they value) and the dangers inherent in the other position (the − quadrant of the opposite pole) gives the participant the freedom and peace to consider additional possibilities. Participants are then able to complete the picture by filling in the other two quadrants in the polarity map.

The need for every individual to complete the picture he or she has of an issue is illustrated by the classic picture in Figure 6.8. Is it a goblet, or is it the profile of two people facing each other? Those who see the goblet image are "right," but when they insist that their view is the only correct perception of the picture, they create an impasse. Similarly, those who see the two people, and insist that those who claim that it is a goblet are "wrong," also create an impasse. It may be true that the picture shows two profiles, but by itself this conclusion is only a half truth. The danger of half-truths is that they are half true, but they are not the whole truth—they do not tell the full story. Polarity Management helps dialogue participants see, or complete, the whole picture. "Paradoxically, opposition becomes resource. The statement becomes, 'I don't see it. You say it's there. Help me see it.' (Johnson, 1992, p. 45)."

Figure 6.8.

4. Polarity Management offers helpful ways for dialogue participants to talk with adversaries (1992, pp. 76–77). Crusaders
   and tradition-bearers are taught to frame their statements in
   ways that elicit a good hearing from adversaries by expressing
   understanding of the other's values and fears, as well as articulating one's own values and fears. For example, a theological
   progressive who is crusading for change would say, "I know
   you think (R+ list) is important. I do too. And I don't want
   to get into (L– list). Yet I also value (L+ list) and am concerned about (R– list)." Similarly, a tradition-bearer from the
   theological conservative side might say, "I hear your concern
   about (R– list) and want to address those concerns too. And
   the points in (L+ list) are valid and important. Yet they make
   me wonder if we can avoid (L– list), because it's important to
   me to preserve (R+ list)."

   The continual movement back and forth between polarities
   represents participants' willingness to see an expanded reality
   and to seriously consider the convictions of the opposite
   polarity. This assures someone on the opposite pole that,
   while you don't want to throw the baby out with the bath
   water (a concern of the tradition-bearer), you are nonetheless
   willing to change the water (a need for the crusader).

5. Polarity Management increases the hope of maximizing the
   upside of each pole. When a concern arises about the downside
   of one of the poles, this is heard as a signal that the group needs
   to move to the upside of the other pole. (Johnson's work elaborates how this is possible.) This will be the church at its best,
   flowing back and forth from strength to strength. In addition,
   as the polarity map takes shape and the flow from strength to
   strength begins, proponents of the two poles will be in a position to identify a higher purpose—a worthy desire embraced by
   both the Left and Right poles. On the lower side of the map,
   participants can join together to embrace a common deeper

fear that both sides want to avoid as they work to stay out of their downside.

The higher purpose and the deeper fear serve as positive and negative purposes for the work of managing the polarity. In the case of the church's progressive-traditionalist polarity, the higher purpose might be to move people toward Christ. Conversely, the deeper fear might be that the downside of the polarity could keep people from Christ (see Figure 6.9).

If it is possible to move toward the higher purpose by pursuing only the upside of the polarity and neglecting its downside, then the conflict is a problem to solve, instead of a polarity to manage. If, as in the issues that continue to divide the church, the growth and health of the church call for an identifying and balancing between the two poles, then the conflict is a polarity to manage.

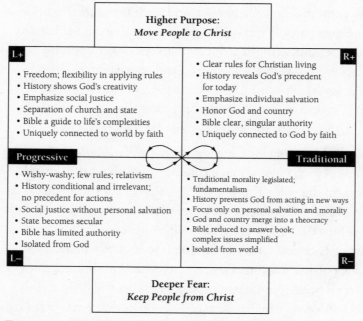

Figure 6.9. The Flow of a Church in Dialogue.
Reprinted from *Polarity Management,* Barry Johnson, 1992. Reprinted by permission of the publisher, HRD Press, Amherst, MA.

As a tool for dialogue, polarity management helps Christians frame the issues that divide us in neutral ways in order for us to deal with them in constructive, hopeful ways.

The following questions may arise for Christians: How does the idea of polarity management and the larger idea of dialogue fit with the central document of our faith? Is dialogue a faithful way of following Christ? Is there any precedent for dialogue from the Bible? Is there any sense in which God engages in dialogue? It is to these questions that we now turn.

7

Hope and the Bible's Invitation to Dialogue

A s Christians, the Bible is our common authority for faith and practice. In our common Book we find models for adversaries coming together in faith and love in order to fulfill the purposes of God. Although the term "dialogue" does not appear in the Bible, we see dimensions of the work we are calling dialogue throughout its pages. These dimensions are not peripheral to the Story of the Bible; to the contrary, they are at the heart of our Book of Faith.

God, the Dialogue Initiator

The Bible records an array of God-human and human-human encounters through which God's intentions for the world are revealed, restated, challenged, misused, and either affirmed or rejected by humans. These encounters are kinds of dialogue. They uncover diversity and create conflicts. Sometimes the diversity and conflict contribute to distrust, distance, even violence. At other times the diversity and conflict produce something new and creative—a dialogue. There is a breakthrough, a transformation. In both the positive and negative encounters, the Bible points to the hope that the God who works in and through human interaction has not given up on transforming this world.

Thus, the Bible witnesses to the never-ending dialogue between God and God's creation, as well as among the creatures, as we try to understand and follow the direction of the Holy One. It is God who initiates dialogue with the people, even in the various struggles between humans, such as in the claiming of territories, in delineating the ceremonially clean and unclean, as well as in weightier matters such as the tensions between law and grace, tradition and prophets, the Jewish leaders and Jesus.

God's people are not simply talking with themselves or to their adversaries in these events. The presence of the Living Lord in their midst causes people to act and enter into these conflicts in the first place. It is God's ways that are being acted out, or rebelled against, and that energize the speech of the people. God is hardly a spectator in these scenes. God is the Logos and Pneuma, the Word and Wind, who gives script and breath to these characters. So it is God's voice we hear through the pages of scripture. God is revealing Godself in the very process of human interactions, as humans struggle and argue to find the wholeness that God desires for us all.

Fortunately, God is not limited to the parameters of our conflicts, for these often lack clarity of discernment. God not only speaks *to* us, but is in dialogue *with* us. When Adam and Eve hide from God in the Garden, God's words invited a response: "Where are you?... Who told you that you were naked?" It is revealing that Adam and Eve got in trouble in the first place because they failed to trust God and to approach God with their own questions. When the serpent cast doubt on God's motives in keeping them from the tree of the knowledge of good and evil ("Did God say...?" "You will not die...." (Genesis 3:1, 4)), Adam and Eve acted on the serpent's alternate suggestion, rather than clarifying their role and relationship with God by going to God for dialogue.

In effect, Adam and Eve ended the dialogue, which ultimately brought their garden experience to an end. Thus Scott Peck defines original sin as the laziness that fails to get God's side of the story before we act. Adam and Eve should have set up a debate between the serpent and God, which would have been "symbolic of the dialogue between good and evil which can and should occur within the minds of human beings" (1978, p. 272).

But God was relentless in initiating dialogue. God sought out Adam and Eve. This God will not rule by Divine edict alone; God invites dialogue as a means of healing and self-understanding. Movement and growth, steps forward and steps backward, occur through dialogue. Thus, the Bible conveys God's relentless hope that through the spirit of dialogue—not by might or by power—the world might know the steadfast love of the Lord. And in this ancient witness, we find our hope and our calling: to play *our* part as agents of God through the holy work of dialogue.

Throughout the Old Testament, God's concern for holiness includes a primary concern with human interactions based in justice. Justice requires relationships of honor and communion between people. These relational qualities are expressed by way of dialogue. Conversely, when dialogue ceases, injustice quickly follows.

For example, the Genesis 4 story of Cain's murder of his brother, Abel, shows anger and jealousy perverting God's plan for life lived in community and dialogue. Cain and Abel were different from each other: Cain was a gardener, and Abel was a sheep herder. When's Abel's offering was accepted by God and Cain's offering was rejected, Cain became jealous. His sense of place and worth were threatened. In order to eliminate the threat of competition, Cain killed his brother. Murder is the ultimate silencing of the dialogue partner's voice, the final refusal to live in a community where every person is valued and every voice heard despite our differences, and where no one but God alone occupies the center. God's swift and severe punishment for this first murder reveals God's utter rejection of the mind-set of Cain. To kill dialogue is to cut ourselves off from God.

This ancient story sets the tone for the remainder of the Old Testament: God's concern is that people act with justice and compassion. Justice comes by way of dialogue. In dialogue, we make room for the those who threaten us. We talk and listen. The call to justice and to dialogue opens up a place in the relationship for the in-breaking of God so that enemies may recognize that, in the end, they are brothers and sisters. When dialogue ceases, then open hands are clenched, injustice reigns, and God is excluded. Conversely, when people are given a voice and their needs are dealt with fairly, God is honored and, in turn, God rewards those who do justice.

The Gospels

Jesus gives specific instruction for followers about what to do when division occurs within the church: "If another member of the church sins against you, go and point out the fault when the two of you are alone. If the member listens to you, you have regained that one. But if you are not listened to, take one or two others along with you, so that every word may be confirmed by the evidence of two or three witnesses" (Matthew 18:15–16).

Jesus' instructions contain a number of elements belonging to our modern understanding of dialogue. The purpose of the dialogue is not to accuse the offender, but to restore the relationship. (For a powerful treatment of this passage, see John Howard Yoder's, *Body Politics*, 1992.) This restoration happens by way of conversation, a dialogue. Followers of Jesus are to be proactive, to take the initiative to go to the other in order to engage in the work of dialogue. The dialogue begins on equal footing, two people talking one-to-one, in private, to allow the offender the opportunity to listen and respond without spectators, so he or she will not lose face in front of the community.

Jesus instructs us to then move to a different strategy if the one-to-one dialogue fails. Take witnesses, says Jesus, which sounds like a concern for safety and self-preservation. But the concern of Jesus in Matthew is for a relentless love for the offender in this work of dialogue. Don't give up, says Jesus. Keep talking. The preceding passage warns against causing another (perhaps our enemy) to stumble

(Matthew 18: 6ff). This is followed by the parable of the shepherd with ninety-nine sheep (12ff) who searches for the one that has gone astray (perhaps the one from whom we are estranged). Next are passages about the relentless quality of Christian forgiveness ("How often should I forgive?" "Seventy times seven."), which goes far beyond the norm of that time to an extravagance that is first demonstrated by God on our behalf. These are not simple or logical admonitions. They are tactics that may be embraced only by followers of Jesus who have first known the profound gift of forgiveness in their own lives.

Jesus' Sermon on the Mount also calls on His followers to enter into dialogue, even when they are not the people who hold the power: "You have heard that it was said, 'An eye for an eye and a tooth for a tooth.' But I say to you, Do not resist an evildoer. But if anyone strikes you on the right cheek, turn the other also; and if anyone wants to sue you and take your coat, give your cloak as well; and if anyone forces you to go one mile, go also the second mile" (Matthew 5: 38–41).

This passage is often heard as an instruction for followers to be passive when someone more powerful wants to dominate them. Instead, Jesus calls followers to create "transforming initiatives" (Stassen, 1983) in relating to our adversaries—taking an initiative that will transform the conflict into a context where growth and perhaps reconciliation are possible.

The "turn-the-other-cheek" admonition is not simply a requirement that we let someone hit us again; it is a call to claim one's worth, to face the oppressor as an equal and to demand to be dealt with accordingly. It initiates an encounter where an oppressor is forced to see the oppressed one as worthy of respect and dialogue.

The "give-the-shirt-off-your-back" admonition is not a requirement to be passive; it challenges the follower to be naked and vulnerable to cause those who are suing you to see the full extent of their action, possibly repent of their oppression, and begin to deal with the oppressed in a redemptive way.

The "go-the-second-mile" admonition does not advocate becoming a doormat for a bully; it is a way to neutralize the dominant ones'

power over you by claiming your own power and making the decision on your own to carry their load further than requested.

In other words, the intent of Jesus' instructions is to empower
His followers to confront their more powerful adversaries in a way
that causes the adversaries to see them in a new light and evokes
their respect. Out of this respect, a transforming dialogue can ensue.

On the heels of these "transforming initiatives," Jesus reminds
His followers, "You have heard that it was said, 'You shall love your
neighbor and hate your enemy.' But I say to you, Love your enemies
and pray for those who persecute you. . . ." (Matthew 5:43–44). His
is a way of reconciliation which requires us to let go of anger, resentment, and vindication, in order to stand together with our enemies
as human beings. To love an enemy *may* transform the enemy. It
does transform the one who loves. It transforms the relationship, if
nowhere else but in the heart of the lover. The words "love" and
"enemy" stand in tension in Jesus' sentence. If love persists, ultimately "enemy" will give way to "friend" or "kindred."

The relentless, reckless love that Jesus focuses on enemies must
be realized within the community of faith itself. Our actions with
the world should also be practiced in the interactions among members of the community. Jesus prays for His followers, " . . . that they
may be one, as we are one. . . ." (John 17:11, 22, 23). This is not a
oneness where questions are banished and differences of opinion
silenced. It is something far deeper. As William Barclay concluded,
"It was not a unity of administration or organization . . . but of personal relationship . . . between heart and heart. Christians will
never organize their Churches all the same way. They will never
worship God all in the same way. They will never even all believe
precisely the same things. But Christian unity transcends all these
differences and joins people together in love" (1955, p. 217).

The story of Jesus taking time to seek out the woman who
touched His hem, to hear her story, to bring healing, has a sacra-
mental and dialogical quality to it. The same is true in other mira-

cle stories and in many of the parables Jesus told. Many of the gospel narratives, as well, can be understood from the framework of dialogue. Jesus' entire life incarnated an ongoing dialogue with God, as well as dialogue with others, both friend and foe. The gospel accounts are told by way of dialogues between Jesus and other people or groups. Throughout the gospels, Jesus is in conflict with His primary adversaries—the Pharisees, the scribes, and even the Devil. He is also in dialogue with those occasional adversaries—His own disciples and followers. They oppose and confound Him. And yet Jesus is in constant communication with them. The dialogue is ongoing, relentless. Jesus never gives up.

Yet Jesus also reminds us that some issues are worth (nonviolently) fighting for: "Do you suppose that I am here to bring peace on earth? No, I tell you, but rather dissension" (Luke 12:51). His stance for justice and true holiness put Him in constant conflict with those who prefer the status quo. The conflicts exposed the need for radical change. To have quelled the conflict through dialogue would have been to neglect the work for which He was sent. (Could this be why Jesus stood silent before Pilate when asked, "What is truth?"?) Jesus had real enemies; his command for us to love our enemies acknowledges their reality and requires a tough love that stands up to them and, through transforming initiatives, hopes to turn them into friends.

Thus for Jesus, a transforming fight was needed. There are fights out there for us too, no doubt. What must be discerned is whether the conflicts that plague the Christian church today are those issues that call for a fight, or whether they are simply presenting issues that call for deeper, more intentional thinking together.

Let us also remember that Jesus' form of fighting differed from the tactics of the world; it involved no violence, a love of enemy in the midst of conflict, and a desire to bring about true peace. And, despite their vast differences, Jesus kept talking with His adversaries throughout His ministry. Jesus never gives up. This One who is the

Word (*logos*) of God is the One through (*dia*) whom God seeks to reconcile the world. God reconciles through the Word: *dia-logos*.

If *dia-logos* is the purpose of God in Jesus Christ, then the work of dialogue in our many divisions within the church is a foundational expression of Christian witness. The work of leaders and laity in trusting the Holy Spirit in dialogue with our adversaries may be the most profound and provocative witness that the church can give to a skeptical world. If the Living Word could empower the church to work at genuine unity *through words* (*dia-logos*), the world, with its own expression of culture wars, will take notice and see the mighty acts of God, even as they did on the day of Pentecost in Acts 2.

The Epistles

The early church was embroiled in conflict shortly after its inception. Acts 6 describes a dispute between the Hellenistic and the Hebrew Christians over the care of Hellenistic widows. Similarly, Acts 15 tells of the ongoing struggle over whether Gentiles could become Christians without first becoming Jews. It is therefore not surprising that as an early church leader, Paul wrote a great deal about the work of dialogue. Many passages could be cited, including the entire book of Ephesians, but following is a sample of Paul's admonitions to engage in what we are calling dialogue:

> So then, putting away falsehood, let all of us speak the truth to our neighbors, for we are members of one another. Be angry but do not sin; do not let the sun go down on your anger, and do not make room for the devil. . . . Let no evil talk come out of your mouths, but only what is useful for building up, as there is need, so that your words may give grace to those who hear. And do not grieve the Holy Spirit of God, with which you

were marked with a seal for the day of redemption. Put away from you all bitterness and wrath and anger and wrangling and slander, together with all malice, and be kind to one another, tenderhearted, forgiving one another, as God in Christ has forgiven you (Ephesians 4:25–27, 29–32).

As God's chosen ones, holy and beloved, clothe yourselves with compassion, kindness, humility, meekness, and patience. Bear with one another and, if anyone has a complaint against another, forgive each other; just as the Lord has forgiven you, so you also must forgive (Colossians 2: 12–13).

Paul's popular words from 1 Corinthians 13, usually associated with weddings and romantic love, are actually part of a letter penned to a church that was deeply divided. The church at Corinth contained factions vying for power. Gluttony reigned at the Lord's table. People competed over which spiritual gift was most important. In this context, Paul reminded the church members, "Love is patient; love is kind; love is not envious or boastful or arrogant or rude. It does not insist on its own way; it is not irritable or resentful; it does not rejoice in wrongdoing, but rejoices in the truth. It bears all things, believes all things, hopes all things, endures all things. Love never ends" (1 Corinthians 13:4–8).

This is a call to a life of dialogue. When Paul returns to the specific issue at hand—the problem caused by speaking in tongues—he continues in the spirit of dialogue: "When you come together, each one has a hymn, a lesson, a revelation, a tongue, or an interpretation. Let all things be done for building up" (14:26). Paul believed that everyone has a gift, and that everyone should have a voice. Church should be a gathering that encourages a dialogue that leads us to a unity of spirit, if not a unanimity of practice or conviction.

Paul's well-known body-of-Christ imagery (I Corinthians 12; Ephesians 4:1–16) illustrates this point: We are not all the same— we are designed for diverse functions that necessitate differing points of view. Eyes are not hands; hands are not feet. What is valuable to hands, for example, soap and water, would be an irritant to the eyes. Even among parts of the body that serve the same function, for example, a set of eyes, there is a difference of viewpoint. Rather than competing with each other, healthy eyes work in tandem to provide the body with a depth perception that is not possible with only one eye.

In Philippians, Paul is again dealing with a conflicted church. Rather than attempting to squelch the conflict, Paul instructs the Philippians about the challenge before them: "If then there is any encouragement in Christ, any consolation from love, any sharing in the Spirit, any compassion and sympathy, make my joy complete: be of the same mind, having the same love, being in full accord and of one mind" (2:1–2).

Could it be that the church is designed to benefit from the dialogue of different viewpoints represented by the Left and Right sides of the invisible line? Could such two-eyed seeing provide a *depth* that cannot be known from the vantage point of the Left eye or the Right eye? Perhaps the oneness that the church should desire is not a oneness of viewpoint, wherein we all see reality as the same and agree on its meaning, but rather the oneness of being a healthy body that incorporates the necessary duality of viewpoints seen from the Left and Right of the Head, who is Christ Himself. Having seen the world from our Left and Right eyes, we report to the Head. Only then, perhaps through the resource of dialogue, can we blend our views and truly "let this mind in (us) that was also in Christ Jesus" (Philippians 2:5).

The call for dialogue is also seen in Paul's letter to the Romans:

> Live in harmony with one another; do not be haughty,
> but associate with the lowly; do not claim to be wiser

than you are. Do not repay anyone evil for evil, but take thought for what is noble in the sight of all. If it is possible, so far as it depends on you, live peaceably with all. Beloved, never avenge yourselves, but leave room for the wrath of God; for it is written, "Vengeance is mine, I will repay, says the Lord." No, "if your enemies are hungry, feed them; if they are thirsty, give them something to drink; for by doing this you will heap burning coals on their heads." Do not be overcome by evil, but overcome evil with good (Romans 12: 16–21).

In Chapters 14 and 15, Paul goes on to deal with a division among groups in the church at Rome whom he describes as the "strong in faith" and the "weak in faith." The "strong in faith" were those who felt no compulsion to obey the Jewish laws regarding what is clean and unclean, who felt free to do what seemed appropriate to them, based on their freedom in Christ. The "weak in faith," on the other hand, retained the structure of the law to guide them in avoiding evil. Hostility had grown between these two understandings of faithful living. Paul's response is a powerful call to the work of dialogue.

Welcome those who are weak in faith, but not for the purpose of quarreling over opinions. Some believe in eating anything, while the weak eat only vegetables. Those who eat must not despise those who abstain, and those who abstain must not pass judgment on those who eat; for God has welcomed them. Who are you to pass judgment on servants of another? It is before their own lord that they stand or fall. And they will be upheld, for the Lord is able to make them stand.

Some judge one day to be better than another, while others judge all days to be alike. Let all be fully convinced in their own minds. Those who observe the day,

observe it in honor of the Lord. Also those who eat, eat
in honor of the Lord, since they give thanks to God;
while those who abstain, abstain in honor of the Lord
and give thanks to God. . . . Let us then pursue what
makes for peace and for mutual upbuilding (Romans
14:1–6, 19).

Like Paul's Lord, there were occasions in his life where prophetic
utterance, not dialogue, was the necessary word, as in his encounter
with Peter at Antioch over Peter's reluctance to be seen with Gentiles (Galatians 2:11–14). At other times, Paul's calling was to give
a reprimand or to end a dispute with a claim to his apostolic authority. And Paul's dialogue skills were sometimes lacking, as we see at
the end of Acts 15, when he and Barnabas disagree over whether
John Mark should go with them. "The disagreement became so
sharp that they parted company. . . . " (15:39). But at his best, Paul
believed that the spirit of dialogue exhibited the spirit of Christ.

To embrace the hope of dialogue is to live in harmony with the
God of the Bible. It is to travel a different way from the way of the
world in which we live. It is to trust that God is not done. Wolves
and lambs will lie down together. The dead will rise. All will see
that "the home of God is among mortals" (Revelation 21:3) because
as the Word becomes incarnate in us, the dialogue continues.
Granted, the way of dialogue can be a rough and lonely way, but
people of hope have the vision to walk this way because we believe
it is the only way, the truth, and the life.

8

Living the Dialogue:
One Church's Story

The following story of dialogue is based on a composite of experiences from churches that have attempted to address one of the most divisive issues of the church today—the relationship between the church and homosexual people. By composing a story, I do not mean to imply that this is a fictitious account. Rather, this story is based on interactions from the churches I have served as well as reports from colleagues around the country. Common experiences have been merged to form one anonymous story.

Many of us are weary of talking about homosexuality and the church. In fact, I hesitated to use it as a topic for modeling dialogue. But the question of the church's response to homosexuality is one of today's most divisive issues. If dialogue is a valuable resource, it must be applied to this crucial question.

This story offers one model for addressing the issue. As this conflict intensifies, more is being written about churches and their experiences in addressing the question. For an excellent sampling of other models of churches addressing homosexuality, see *Congregations Talking About Homosexuality* (Gaede, 1998).

As you will see, dialogue is no magic elixir for solving the conflict. The goal of dialogue is not to come to agreement, but to deepen and temper the conversation into a meaningful interaction where God's Spirit can flow.

· · · · · · ·

No one was surprised when Richard was placed in a leadership position by his church. Richard was articulate, energetic, and had a keen vision for the future of the church. Last year Richard gave a moving testimony of his conversion experience as part of a morning worship service that touched the hearts of many in the congregation and sparked a small revival. He was especially popular in several circles within the church—the young people with whom he had worked on weekend youth events, the members of the choir with whom he sang, and the senior adults he shuttled to and from services each week in the church van. It seemed that Richard was as close to an ideal member as a church could hope to find.

When rumors began to circulate about Richard's sexual orientation, it caused considerable waves within the church. And Richard's recent acknowledgment of his homosexuality after being confronted by a member rocked the church to its core. Richard? How could this be? What should we do? Should Richard still be allowed to function in the roles he's played in the past? Or should he be relieved of all leadership responsibilities and banned from singing in the choir?

Many members didn't know what to think or do. This was the first time they had been confronted with the question of homosexuality on such a personal basis. The issue was already being debated at the denomination's national level. It came up for vote in city elections with some regularity. Now it had come to their church, but in this case the members found that the issue was less clear—it was one thing to make generalized judgments about homosexuals based on scripture or their own personal reaction to the concept, but quite another to consider Richard, their friend and coworker in ministry, and to frame the issue in ways that excluded him. They felt torn by two competing allegiances—faith and friendship—and simply refused to take a stand.

Other members avoided the issue because it made them uncomfortable. They did not like talking about heterosexuality, much less this different kind of sexuality they could not relate to. "Do we have to talk about this?" they asked.

Others took a live-and-let-live approach. "What Richard does in the privacy of his home is his business, not the church's and certainly not any individual's in the church," they said. "Besides, the Bible's understanding of homosexuality is so antiquated that it is irrelevant, not to mention that science continues to break new ground suggesting that homosexuality is a condition, not a choice."

Some accepted the possibility that a person could be homosexual, but they thought that a person with this condition should resist it. For this group, there was nothing sinful about being homosexual; the sin was in acting on those sexual desires.

Still others believed that to deviate from the Bible was to turn one's back on God, who has lovingly given the world the parameters in which to live. Homosexuality falls outside these parameters of wholeness, they believed. Thus, as much as they loved Richard, their love and loyalty to God needed to come first. In fact, it was because of their love for Richard that they were adamant about naming homosexuality as a sin. How else can Richard be led from this destructive lifestyle? "It is a heart-breaking decision," said one of the leaders. "We wish that we didn't have to make it. But we simply must take action to remove Richard from visibility in the life of the church. How else will he and others know how important it is to let God heal them from this disease?"

Members began lining up on a continuum of views on the issue, with Richard in the center of the fray, confused and embarrassed. Many members retreated to the sidelines, either unable or unwilling to choose a side. Those who chose sides had one thing in common: Both viewed the conflict as a battle for the soul of the church—one side fighting for adherence to the teachings of the Bible and the church's historical stance against homosexuality, the other side fighting for adherence to the *spirit* of the Bible and strong but fluid values that can be adapted to changes in culture and science over time.

Participants from both sides felt pressured to speak not only for their own deepest convictions, but also in some way to represent a larger constituency outside the congregation who desired a certain outcome from the conflict. "This victory is essential for our side," both sides of the conflict were told. "You must take a firm stand and refuse to let the other side dissuade you."

Opponents of homosexuality contended that to allow an avowed homosexual to continue in church leadership was the same as condoning this sinful lifestyle. "Homosexuality is simply not in God's plan, and the Bible is clear about that." They also feared what might follow if Richard were allowed to remain in leadership. "First you grant them a place, then they want acceptance, then they want their relationships blessed by the church. This will undermine the church's teaching on marriage, which is what our entire society is based on. Then they'll want to be ordained to lead the church." Phone calls and letters began to come in from individuals and groups within their denomination opposing homosexuality. "There must be no compromise. You must hold to traditional denominational teachings, or risk expulsion."

The other side emphasized Richard's unquestionably moral and exemplary lifestyle (Richard's recent disclosure notwithstanding). "If Richard isn't a follower of Jesus, who is? Besides, if we're going to start disqualifying sinners from leadership positions, what about those in our church who are divorced, or overweight, or supportive of immoral military actions? Are we going to begin auditing members' tax returns to make sure no one cheats?" Advocates of a more open society pressured Richard's supporters to lead the church to be more tolerant, more inclusive of all people without judging their lifestyles. "If your church doesn't take a stand of tolerance, you will be known as bigots, mental dinosaurs, and homophobes, no better than the KKK. Remember, the Bible says, 'Judge not, that you be not judged.'"

The most vocal and adamant from both sides prepared for battle. Books were read. Experts consulted. Research documented.

Position papers were drawn up. A date for the church meeting was set.

As the meeting approached, Richard considered removing himself from the conflict and voluntarily leaving the church. He wondered if the issue would be too divisive for the good of the church. He also wondered if the struggle to retain his place in the church was worth the price that it would cost either him or the church. In addition, Richard's doctor told him that the pressure of the issue was one of the causes for his recurring battle with depression. "Maybe I should just go to the Metropolitan Community Church where I know I'm wanted and accepted," he said. His friends in the church argued for him to see the conflict through, but some of them were secretly relieved that the battle might be averted and that things could get back to normal again at church.

Richard decided to meet concerned members of the church halfway. He offered to take a sabbatical from leadership in the church, but also asked that the church use this time to engage in a careful churchwide exploration of the issues surrounding the question of homosexuals and the church. The pastor and lay leadership thought this was a reasonable request and agreed.

Pastor Mark was a theological conservative. Typically, he let the Bible end discussions on matters of disagreement. He knew the biblical passages that prohibit homosexuality and accepted them as true; if the Bible said it, that settled it. But when the particular passages were applied to Richard, he felt a twinge of discomfort with his usual unequivocal approach. To say that Richard would not inherit the kingdom of God, as it said in I Corinthians, simply didn't ring right for Mark. His ambivalence confused him.

In addition, it seemed to him that every option before him had a significant downside. If he came down on the side of Richard and said he could remain in leadership, he would draw the ire of a sizable part of the church, including one strongly opposed family whose gifts to the church were purported to represent over ten percent of the total budget. He would also face the condemnation of his denomination and might even risk being dismissed. Worst, he worried if this option meant he no longer believed that the Bible was the inspired word of God.

Another option, to ignore or avoid the situation, felt cowardly and probably wouldn't work at that point anyway. Even if it did, it was likely that it would leave an open wound that would fester in the darkness.

Some church leaders advocated having a debate on the issue, where side would present its case, followed by a point-counterpoint exchange and a final vote by the congregation. Pastor Mark agreed that this was the most logical approach, but he suspected that this option would polarize the church even further and would likely be a fiasco with little room for the Spirit to move.

Another group within the church contended that the best the church could hope for in such a situation was compromise: for example, let Richard remain as a choir member, but remove him from any leadership role or contact with children or young people. "We'll love the sinner, but not condone the sin," they said.

Others wanted to hire an outside consultant skilled in conflict management to help the church resolve the conflict. Something in Pastor Mark's gut told him that such an approach wouldn't allow the church to deal in depth with the issue, but would only focus the concern on getting the church get past the conflict.

Pastor Mark had another concern: as pastor, what role should *he* play in this conflict? Should he remain neutral and let the church decide the issue? Or was it time for him to exert leadership by declaring a position based on his own study of the issue and conclusions?

"No option feels right. It seems like a no-win situation," he said to Ted, a clergy friend at a nearby church, as he reviewed all the ways to approach the conflict brewing in his church.

Ted thought for several minutes. "I've heard of some conflicted groups being helped in dealing with their problems by using the approach of dialogue."

Mark was doubtful. "Dialogue sounds like people talking civilly and rationally to each other. Our most entrenched members won't do that. If I suggest that we sit down to talk together about our differences, the staunch conservatives will say I'm giving room for the other side to maneuver their way in; and the staunch liberals will say I'm not being bold enough."

"You're right," agreed Ted. "Dialogue won't satisfy the most ardent people in your church. In fact, unlike other forms of conflict management, dialogue doesn't even attempt to fix the problem. Its purpose is simply to create an atmosphere where new possibilities other than win-lose or yes-no can be explored with integrity by all parties. If anything, dialogue takes a church deeper into the problem. But it is like going deeper into a funnel—the deeper you go, the closer you get to each other, and the closer you come to a common ground where you can work together."

Mark shook his head. "I don't see that working. You know the folks in my church: They are rational, results-oriented. They are problem solvers. Dialogue will sound to them like wallowing around in the problem, rather than trying to fix it."

"That's a challenge," Ted admitted. "Dialogue forces participants to be out of control for a while, to suspend their judgments, and to listen for the collective wisdom that emerges from the group. It's a tough process for management-type people. Maybe it won't work. But what have you got to lose? Maybe getting such radically conflicted people together can create something new and dynamic. Maybe that's why Jesus called both Matthew the tax collector as well as Simon the Zealot to be in the same small group of disciples. Maybe they need each other to keep things stirred up. I heard somewhere that the fish industry found that the secret for keeping live tuna from getting mushy and dormant while being transported in tanks was to throw in a catfish—the enemy of the tuna—to keep them moving around!"

"That's all we need," mourned Mark, "a church full of people who can't relax for fear another member is going to bite them!"

"O.K., maybe it's not a perfect analogy, but you get the point: remaining connected with people with whom we disagree keeps us on our toes and avoids the idea that conflict is bad because the church is about everyone agreeing on every issue."

"There is another problem," said Mark. "How in the world can the church deal with such an explosive issue in the midst of all the other activities scheduled for the coming months? New study classes have already begun; soon it will be budget and stewardship time again, not to mention the holidays."

"I hear you," sympathized Ted. "There never seems to be a good time for these kinds of unplanned crises to pop up. They interrupt us and knock us off course. But these kind of things sure seem to happen in every dynamic church I know."

"I used a quote by Carl Jung last Sunday in my sermon," recalled Mark: "'Do not despise the interruptions of life; every interruption is an interruption from God.' Maybe this is one of those moments."

When the conflict over Richard arose, Pastor Mark's first reaction was to schedule a series of presentations to the entire church where he could lay out the various issues related to homosexuality, along with his conclusions, since a few years earlier he had done extensive research on this topic. But as he considered the wisdom of leading the church in this way, it occurred to Mark that since he had developed some strong personal convictions on the subject, he might not be able to give a fair and objective presentation on the various positions held by other Christians.

In addition, although Pastor Mark didn't mind taking unpopular stands on issues, he recognized that if he came across as a spokesperson for one particular side, then his ability to relate pastorally to the other side would be diminished. After much prayer, Mark concluded that this was not an occasion to lead by taking a particular stand and calling the church to line up behind him. Rather, he recognized that his role in this controversy was to lead by empowering the congregation to dialogue together and to discern the best course of action as a body to the best of their ability.

Mark began by learning all he could about dialogue—its principles and its pitfalls. The more he read about the nature of dialogue and the possibilities that it creates, the more convinced he was that this method could give the church the resources that it needed to creatively address the question of homosexuality.

Mark went to the church's lay leadership to propose the idea of a congregational dialogue. He laid out the unique dimensions of dialogue and answered their questions about how it would work as best he could. When the leaders seemed willing to try a dialogue, Pastor Mark asked them to join him in proposing this course of action to the church, to lead the church in the process by overseeing the dialogue, and to pledge their prayers and attendance at the dialogue gatherings.

The next step, he suggested, was to create an ad hoc dialogue group to develop the process that the church would use. He suggested that representatives with strong feelings from both sides of the issue, as well as people who felt caught in the middle, be included in the planning of the process. Mark offered several different models for the process, along with their pros and cons, but the final decision for how the church would proceed was left up to the group.

"Remember," he said, "we can't program or guarantee the outcome of a dialogue. We have to trust the process, trust each other, and trust that God's Spirit will use our open hearts and minds."

It felt providential to Pastor Mark that the text for the following Sunday was from Paul's thoughts about unity in diversity from I Corinthians (12: 20–21): ("As it is, there are many members, but one body. The eye cannot say to the hand, 'I have no need of you,' nor again the head to the feet 'I have no need of you.'"). Mark reminded the church that the point of a body is not uniformity, but unity. "Let us attack the questions together, rather than attack each other. Let's work as a team," he urged.

That week, representatives from the ad hoc dialogue group went to the most vocal members of both sides to solicit their support for a dialogue and to identify what ground rules and setting would help them feel comfortable in entering into a dialogue. This information was taken to the ad hoc group's meeting and used as input in forming a set of guidelines for the congregation's discussions.

The ad hoc group was interested to note that both sides of the issue had a sizable number of people who refused to consider dialogue. For them, the issue was so clear and unambiguous that they viewed dialogue as compromise. The group representative had reminded them, "The goal of dialogue is not to compromise, but to see if something new can come from sharing our deepest convictions with each other in a context of love and respect."

In many cases, the most strident still refused. "This is the kind of moral relativism that is destroying our country," argued those who opposed homosexuality. "We must stand up for what's right, for the Bible and absolute truth." Five families announced that they were leaving the church immediately as a result of the decision to discuss the topic. The effect of their departure would be significant, both in leadership and in financial support. "We can't afford to lose many more like them," warned the church treasurer.

There was also a negative, though less strident, reaction to the dialogue decision on the other side of the continuum. "Why should we have to discuss whether or not the church approves of us?" asked several gay members. "Are we going to have future dialogues about other kinds of alleged sin committed by heterosexuals?" "I've fought about sexual orientation at home and at work. I'm not fighting about it anymore," said four members, who quit attending the church.

Still others left the church even though they were less personally invested in the topic. "We don't want to attend a church in conflict. We just want to worship and witness, and leave the fighting to someone else."

Reports of the various departures left Mark and the rest of the leadership feeling betrayed and doubtful. Was dialogue the right course of action? Had they discerned the Spirit's leading, or were they forcing an issue that could do serious damage to their church? If this was the effect of simply deciding to talk about homosexuality, what could they expect as they made progress on the issue? There were several sleepless nights among the leaders, but they agreed to go forward.

Later that week, Pastor Mark sent a letter to the entire church family concerning the conflict, encouraging full participation in the dialogue from every member. It said, "This question of the place of homosexual people in a Christian church is a legitimate point of disagreement. A continuing debate about precisely what the Bible says and means about homosexuality continues to this day among devout and respected scholars in the church. This is not purely an academic debate. Our church now faces the issue in a personal way, because it is before us in the form of an active member of this church.

"Because we are a church where the Bible is authoritative and where, under Christ, everyone's voice matters, this is an issue that requires the community to discern the mind of Christ and to find a way for us to live together in peace. This is a unique opportunity for the church to deepen our understanding of a complex issue; to forge a more profound sense for us to be one in spite of our different views; and to show others how Christ can guide us in ways of peace."

The next week the adult Sunday school hour was spent in a churchwide presentation on dialogue. Also presented were a set of guidelines agreed to by the church's ad hoc dialogue group. Members were then urged to participate in one of the many dialogue groups. In a church of 800 it was impossible for all members to talk as a single group; yet the leaders felt it was important for the church to have a singular kind of community experience. A combination of large-group presentations and small-group dialogues that would be held in various members' homes were designed.

Members registering for the small groups indicated whether they supported, opposed, or were undecided about homosexuals in church. Groups were then formed to ensure a variety of views in each group. Each group was assigned a recorder who summarized the various responses given at each session. These responses were submitted to a lay leader, who merged them into a single list that was published in the following week's church newsletter, so the entire church could get a feel for the range of views being expressed.

John was one of the deacons and other willing leaders who agreed to be trained to facilitate a healthy, vibrant dialogue. John had been a deacon for eight years, but this role of moderating a dialogue group was the most daunting task he had ever been asked to undertake by the church.

After his dialogue group settled in to the refreshments, he began by asking participants to share their name, how long they had been involved in the church, and what they loved about their church. A few times John gently interrupted a response that went on too long or was too far afield. When all had spoken, John led in prayer.

"Now let's go around the room with each person reading one of the Guidelines for Dialogue that have been agreed on by our organizing group."

John then offered a few suggestions. "Some of us are more vocal than others, and our thoughts are formed into words more quickly. In order to ensure everyone has an opportunity to speak, those who are more vocal will need to monitor the number of times you speak and the length of your talk. I also encourage those who are less vocal to monitor your silence and to bring your thoughts into words for the group.

"Also, we're going to use this carpet sample to indicate which of us has 'the floor.' If you want to speak, ask for the floor. It's the group's job to help regulate itself and to let only the person who has the floor speak.

"Here are four questions for us to consider over the next two nights. Let's all answer one question before we go on to the next one:"

1. How do you relate to the question of homosexuality from your own life experience?

2. What is the essential faith value for you that is touched by the question of homosexuality?

3. What concerns or worries do you have for our church as we enter this dialogue?

4. What hopes do you have for our church as we enter this dialogue?

The sharing was slow at first. But as people began to explore the question, others got a clearer idea of what was being asked and how to frame a response. Twice the group had to remind people that they didn't "have the floor." It was done with humor and was received well, but it kept the conversation orderly and deliberate.

There were significant differences in experiences and positions. Frank said he'd never met a homosexual; others knew homosexual people, but not well; a few had gay friends. Finally, Carol, a middle-aged woman took the carpet and said to Frank, "You say you don't know a homosexual. Well, now you do. I'm gay." She told the group it was the first time she'd ever said those words to a group of people. A powerful silence filled the room.

The essential faith value also varied within the group, as did the hopes and concerns. People who opposed homosexuality spoke of keeping the church free from sin, or of concern for young people and the message an acceptance of homosexuality sends to them. These views created considerable discomfort for those who supported homosexuals in the church. The tension was evident in their faces and voices. Others expressed the importance of preserving the strength and reputation of the church. Still others spoke of the call to justice and liberation, compassion, love, and of erring on the side of grace. Those who opposed homosexuals in the church squirmed at this kind of language.

As the second meeting ended, John said, "I wonder if there is a common value that we can agree that all of us are trying to honor as our highest value." Group members listed several phrases: be fair; do the right thing; follow the Bible; restore peace in the church. Someone suggested "glorify God" and again a thoughtful silence filled the room.

"Can we agree that the higher purpose that each of us has in all of our discussion and differences of views is to glorify God?" asked John.

There was a moment's hesitancy from strong supporters on either side, but finally there was a nod of yes. "I don't always see it in the other side, and I sure don't feel it from them," one admitted. "But I trust that is what they are about."

"Perhaps that is the first piece of our common ground," offered John. "Let's end by joining hands and praying The Lord's Prayer."

The following week the church met together to hear the first of two presentations on the Bible and homosexuality. The ad hoc dialogue group had decided some weeks earlier to have these presentations, and it had not been an easy decision. Views varied on whether it would be a helpful addition to the discussion.

"I think it's important that we hear from some experts on the subject," said Bill. "Getting people together will help to defuse the anger, but it won't get us into the real heart of the issue; namely, what does the Bible say about homosexuality? I sure hope we're not going to avoid getting deep into scripture on this topic. We need to confront some of the misunderstandings that I've been hearing about what the Bible says on this subject."

"Your desire to explore the Bible's teachings on the subject is legitimate," said Linda, another member of the ad hoc group, "although I must admit it makes me nervous. My fear is that bringing in so-called experts will throw the dialogue into a debate."

"If we're not willing to argue over what the Bible says, what are we doing here?" asked Bill.

"I'm not sure this will help us 'argue' constructively over what the Bible says," answered Linda. "I'm afraid that it would turn into a dueling-Bibles match. Each side will bring in their experts; the experts will throw out a lot more arguments than any of us can assimilate; both sides' experts will refute the position of the other. How will we know who to believe?"

"Is there any way we can present the different views without turning it into a my-scholar-can-whip-your-scholar kind of contest?" asked Steve.

"Maybe the real concern is what our folks do with the presentations," said Jan. "If we can help people move beyond simply saying, 'I disagree with that scholar' or 'I vote for that one' and help them get at what rings more true or false to them, then the presentations can have a constructive contribution to our dialogues. In fact, I wonder if the ways we've been taught to communicate for these dialogues might put us in a position to hear and apply the different views of experts in ways that could deepen the conversation, rather than polarize it further."

After considerable discussion, the ad hoc dialogue group decided to schedule speakers to present differing views on the Bible and homosexuality. House groups were scheduled to meet again after both presentations had been given. It was agreed that, in order to encourage careful listening to the speakers and discourage members from debating the speakers, the pastor would moderate the question-and-answer period at the close of the presentations and would take only questions that sought clarification on a point, rather than questions that argued or challenged.

As expected, both presenters made compelling cases for the accuracy of their positions: one contended that the Bible teaches that practicing homosexuality is incompatible with a virtuous Christian life; the other contended that the Bible's view of homosexuality must be interpreted in the larger cultural context in which it was written and, as a result, does not apply directly to homosexuality as we understand it in today's culture.

At the outset of each presentation, church members were given a list of questions, prepared by the organizing group, to consider as they listened to the presentations. The questions were framed to invite deeper listening to the presenters and to encourage exploring the issue from the presenters' understanding of the issue.

1. According to the presenter, what are the key points we need to consider? What, for the presenter, is the essential faith value that is touched by the question of homosexuality?

2. Whether you agree with the presenter's conclusions or not, what valid points were raised that you agree should be part of the church's consideration as we deal with this issue?

3. What new insights did you hear?

4. What points did you expect to hear, but didn't?

At Deacon John's next group meeting, the participants were more than ready to talk about what they'd heard. John reminded them that the goal was not to win or lose a debate, but to allow the conversation to take them to a new and deeper understanding of the topic. Some members were uncomfortable conceding any valid points by the presenters whose views opposed theirs. Careful, gentle leadership by John prodded the group to think through each position and to go beyond weighing the evidence to exploring the assumptions made by the speakers, the values that shaped the presentation, and ways the speakers joined the group in their highest value of "glorifying God."

Two weeks after the two Bible presentations, the church met as a whole with Pastor Mark as moderator to hear a thirty-minute summary of the two presentations, based on the group recorders' reports from the house groups. It was helpful to hear unique insights gleaned from some groups as well as the common themes picked up by most of the groups. (Meeting organizers also planned refreshments and fun skits about upcoming church events to remind everyone that the conflict over homosexuality was not the single issue in the church's life.)

The rest of the churchwide meeting was used to make a presentation of Polarity Management™. At the conclusion, the following assignment was given for the next house group meetings:

1. Is the question of homosexuality and Christianity a problem to be solved or a polarity to be managed? Is it possible to characterize each of the poles in a neutral way?

2. Draw a polarity map of the issue that includes the strengths and weaknesses of both polarities. (Note that this was the first time that participants were invited to speak to the weakness of the positions.)

3. Does the map designed by the group illustrate the conflict in a way that satisfies everyone in the group? If not, how should it be altered? Does it aid the dialogue? Does it bring us to resolution?

As the members adjourned, Pastor Mark couldn't help but notice that some of the staunchest members on either side of the issue had dropped out of the process. He wondered if the process of dialogue had been too conciliatory or too tedious for them. While he was saddened by their decision to be absent, he recognized that, given the intransigence of their positions, dialogue would feel more like commiserating with the enemy than a meaningful exercise in Christian community.

The creation of the polarity maps was a powerful experience for most of the groups. As participants worked together, they found the freedom both to acknowledge the strengths of the other side, to name the strengths of their own side, and to (finally!) offer a critique of the other side. Perhaps most importantly, the safety of the dialogue around the polarity maps was a place where participants were invited to confide the places of uncertainty or conflict in their own positions.

When the map was complete, John's group sat silently as they looked at their creation—a map depicting the conflict that had dominated their church's life for the past three months. It felt both strange and comforting to see the issue laid out in such a graphic manner.

Finally Joan spoke. "This helps me see the bigger picture. It doesn't feel as much like an either-or question to me as it did when we began," she said. "I don't feel as strongly about either converting or silencing those who disagree with me. That just causes more heat and polarization. I'm still personally uncomfortable with homosexuality, and I still want to persuade others to my view, but I'm not as convinced that I need to force my view on others, or maybe even on the church."

Les took the floor, "I have to admit that I've got more questions now than I did before. It's harder to make blanket statements about gays, now that I know a gay person. It reminds me of the recent case of the woman on death row in Texas. People like Pat Robertson, who strongly support the death penalty, got to know that woman. It caused them to ask some hard questions about capital punishment, which they strongly supported before they got to know her."

Darlene, one of Richard's friends, responded, "I've had a similar experience in hearing those of you who oppose Richard's continued leadership in the church. I assumed that you actually enjoyed pointing a finger at a 'sinner' and excluding him from our church's leadership. It's obvious to me now that this is not easy for you. You care about people. But you see homosexuality as a sin that has to be overcome, like addiction. That casts the issue in a different light for you. With that assumption, I can see why Richard serving in a leadership capacity would raise some concerns for you."

Ken spoke up. "My main concern still has to do with the reputation of our church. We've been a strong, family-oriented church in this community for 100 years. If we take a stand that opens the door to gays, it will split this church and damage its reputation in the community. People will think we're a bunch of liberals. We're not liberal, and I don't want to do anything that compromises the future or the reputation of this church."

Carol responded to Ken, "As we've talked these past weeks, I've come to see why the reputation of the church is the most important concern for you. You're trying to protect something you love and value, namely the church, from the fallout of a battle that isn't even yours. I can't fault you for that. Homosexuality isn't a burning issue for you like it is for some of us. For us, though, it is a justice issue and feels worth pursing at any cost."

Ken took the piece of carpet and thought for several moments, "I wish we could work together to balance all our concerns: working for justice, honoring Biblical truth, and preserving the reputation and health of our church. I don't like choosing between those options. They're all important to me."

Darlene took the carpet from Ken. "Ken, I think you just expressed the feelings of a lot of us. We're all looking for a way to think and work together through this issue to obtain the kind of spiritual balance that addresses our deepest values and glorifies God."

Carol spoke up. "Has anyone noticed that we've had heated, passionate discussions, but never really harsh words? I think that's because we like and respect each other. At least I can say that I like all of you."

"Well, I like you too," said Frank, who had opposed including homosexuals in active church life. He paused. "You have to understand where I come from. Everything I've learned in my life is the opposite of this homosexual stuff. Seeing homosexuals as good Christians simply conflicts with all that I know to be true. It's difficult for me to open up to see things in a new light, even if I wanted to. I'm having to acknowledge—no matter what the Bible says about the sin of your sexual activity—that gays are people just like me."

"Frank, I want you to know that I've learned something from you," said Mike, who was supportive of gay members. "By your devotion to scripture, you've reminded me of how important it is that we honor God's word. I think of the Apostle Paul's statement about being "tossed about by every wind of deceit . . ." and think: Is that me? I'm not comfortable saying that everything is relative, or that there aren't any absolutes. Even though my experience and interpretation lead me to remove today's understanding of homosexuality from the list of prohibitions, I still think there are many absolutes that the Bible shows us. I sure don't want to throw out the baby with the bath water."

"That's good to hear. I appreciate you saying that," said Frank. He turned to Carol. "I remember the night you told us that you had to put your dog to sleep the previous week. I remember thinking, 'I had a dog die recently.' Then later that same night you also mentioned that you'd gotten a Valentine from your Mom. That struck me, because my Mom still sends me Valentines too. I thought, in a way, we're a lot alike: two people trying to live our lives as best as we know how."

Phil agreed. "I'm realizing that just as I hate it when people stereotype me with leaders like Jerry Falwell just because I'm an evangelical, in the same way it's unfair for me to lump all homosexuals together and imply that they're all like the most outrageous gays in San Francisco. Evangelicals aren't all the same, and I guess neither are gays. I'm not sure what difference that makes, if I believe that the Bible says homosexuality is wrong, but somehow it does make a difference. It makes it hard to know what is right."

The group was silent again. Mike broke the silence. "I know most of us would like to resolve this issue, for Richard's sake and for the church's. I'm personally ready to accept gays into church leadership. But since members of the church interpret the Bible and homosexuality in different ways, I wonder if we could just agree to continue together in ministry while this question is still being explored, no matter how long it takes. Would the church be willing to live with the ambiguity of not deciding, while we continue to talk together and to trust that the Holy Spirit can shape us if we are truly open? It seems to me that we've made significant progress simply by talking about the issue. Apparently it's not a new issue or one that the universal church has been able to resolve quickly. Why do we think that we have to make a firm decision one way or the other?"

He continued. "In the meantime, what if the church left Richard's leadership roles up to the particular groups that call forth leaders? People can vote their conscience at that time. Some will believe that Richard is qualified; others won't. If he's elected to leadership, those who don't think he's qualified will need to accept it as the will of the congregation for that position. Frankly, I've had to do that with people whom I didn't consider qualified for leadership based on their business ethics and level of spiritual maturity. It's part of being a church together. If I want to be in a church that I agree with 100 percent of the time, I'd be able to hold church in a phone booth."

Carol turned to Mike. "I don't like leaving the issue open, because it means I know I'll be sitting in church with people who continue to vote against gays in leadership just because they're gay. That feels pretty uncomfortable. But I have to recognize that people who believe that faithful Christians can't be gay would be making a major concession too. I suppose we could avoid this discomfort by segregating ourselves. Heterosexuals could ban us from their churches and gays could flock to the gay church. It would be easier, but it doesn't sound like the kind of church that Christ had in mind."

"It doesn't to me either," said Frank. "Even though I think that the Bible says homosexuality is wrong, I don't want to kick gays out of the church. But because of what I believe, I'm still uncomfortable with gays in church leadership."

"I'm thankful to have a context where discussion, not debate or winning, is the goal," said John. "These discussions aren't making the question of what to do with Richard any easier. If anything, they make the issue more complex, but at the same time, for me, much richer and more complete. I like what we're doing, and look forward to our next meeting."

9

When God Enters Our Conflicts

The world to which Christian faith gives its witness is full of polarities and conflicting agendas. An "on the one hand . . ." is followed by an equally compelling "on the other hand . . ." in virtually every arena of life—in nature, business, relationships, politics, education, technology, community development, law, and environmental concerns. So it should neither surprise nor disappoint Christians that our faith world has similar polarities—theological and methodological "on the one hands" that dominate (at worst) or stand alongside (at best) the "on the other hands" of our faith world. Basic polarities exist, such as grace and works, law and gospel. Doctrinal polarities also exist, such as God's transcendence and immanence, Jesus' humanity and divinity, humanity's duality of body and spirit, our sinfulness and our being made in God's image, the Kingdom's now and not yet, the Word as flesh and the Word as words, God's justice and God's mercy.

These polarities permeate the life of the church: discipline and spontaneity, individuality and community, stability and change, the open and closed fellowship of the church. Christian polarities shape our life of obedience, calling us to be drawn simultaneously by both revelation and reason, trusting and trying, self-sacrifice and self-love, serving God out of gratitude or for rewards.

Then there are the legions of questions that come from our reading of scripture: Jesus tells us to love the world; in another verse He says to hate the world. On one occasion He says He is the light of the world; on another He calls us the light of the world. What exactly is Christ's body—Jesus, or the church? Is Christ "with you always," or is He coming again?

Yet both progressives and traditionalists are prone to act as if Jesus rid the world of polarities. In Him, we imply, there ought not be the tension between "on the one hand . . ." and "on the other hand. . . ." Surely there is a right and a wrong, we say, and the call of the gospel is to discern the right from the wrong and become its champion for Christ.

Creating Something New

Dialogue serves as an invitation for Christians to understand the world as it is, to hear its many competing claims, and to feel its tensions within our own skin. It is an invitation to something new—a world of dialogue where we have an opportunity to play a part in the creative balancing that Christ calls us to undertake through sustained conversations with our adversaries.

This world of dialogue recognizes that differences among us—call them polarities, dualities, or paradoxes—are built into the fabric of creation. Dialogue invites Christians to confront our differences from a different angle: by working through our differences to explore the deeper issues of life, rather than simply working to overcome our surface distinctions without delving deeper to discover the substantive differences between us.

For example, dialogue does not deny the reality of sin. We know that all human beings separate themselves from God by our rejection of God's ways. Christians believe that in Jesus Christ we have been given access by God to restore the sin-impaired relationship. But conflicts arise among Christians over different understandings of humanity's separation from God. Faithful Christians have differing views of what constitutes sin, what is a faithful lifestyle for

Christians, what the church ought to say to the world's many polarities, and how to apply the message of the Bible to today's world.

Dialogue invites participants into a deeper conversation about sin, its nature and its implications. It allows participants to look at sin both as a particular action and also as a more general attitude, as a specific event and as a condition of the context in which we were born. These two expressions of sin are both complimentary and contradictory—they are necessary polarities. One without the other loses its effectiveness, its power to transform the human heart. Dialogue demands that we keep a harmony between these two understandings of sin in order to glean the best from both of them.

Dialogue seeks this same interplay between all the polarities that are important to our understanding of life as Christians. In this way, dialogue serves the church by going far beyond assuaging our conflicts. It leads the church into fully examining tensions and in recognizing that these tensions are necessary for balance to be maintained and for the truth that transcends opposing sides to break forth.

Dialogue as a Way of Life

Dialogue at its best becomes far more than a methodology for handling conflicts among Christians. It becomes a way of life that enables us to relate to people whose views differ from ours with both reverence toward other people and diligence about one's own conviction. Missionaries around the globe have embodied this way of life for many years. They bear witness to their experience of the gospel and the nature and mystery of the Holy, while they also listen to the experiences and traditions of those they speak to.

As a way of life, dialogue becomes a discipline leading to higher levels of spirituality. The Guidelines for Dialogue first suggested in Chapter Three move us into a world that cultivates higher levels of Christian maturity.

1. Risk is moving beyond our fears of the unknown and trusting that God will be there to undergird us.

2. Respect is granting that the image of God is present in all people and being willing to grant them this honored place, even when we cannot see it in them with our own eyes.

3. Fairness is releasing the temptation to get the upper hand by any means available, and trusting the process enough to grant an adversary a level playing field for the give and take of ideas.

4. Humility is owning one's limitations in every area of life.

5. Teamwork is looking for the Holy Spirit in the most unexpected of places.

6. Openness is being willing to learn.

7. Listening is recognizing that God is at work in other places.

8. First-person speech is recognizing that God is at work in you.

9. Depth is believing that God's truth has levels of complexity and meaning that humanity will never fully comprehend.

10. Patience is understanding that we are part of a long lineage of people who have sought to discern the will of God in community, and finding the grace to humbly play our part.

Dialogue emerges from *agape* love, a self-giving commitment to the spiritual growth of another (Peck, 1978, p. 60ff). Thus the work of dialogue is, finally, a spiritual endeavor that yields great spiritual rewards. It is an act of "communion in which we are mutually informed, purified, illumined, and reunited to ourselves, to one another, and to God[:] . . . a condition and relationship for the appearance and work of the Spirit" (Howe, 1963, p.106). In dialogue, hope is born, or perhaps more accurately, kept alive. To enter into dialogue is to act in the hope that God will be present to help us overcome the barriers between us. Dialogue claims the promises of God that we can rise above the despair of our divisions.

In 1953, only a decade after the Holocaust, Jewish philosopher Martin Buber was awarded a prize by the German Book Traders. His speech was strained as he addressed this assembly of German thinkers on the topic of "Genuine Dialogue and the Possibilities of Peace." Buber spoke of the horrible events of the past decade and of the need to continue to speak in the face of these incomprehensible events. "To speak," he said, "is a sign of hope. . . . Fighting begins where speech has ceased," he told the audience. Buber concluded, "The name 'Satan' means in Hebrew 'the hinderer'. That is the correct designation for the anti-human in individuals and in the human race. Let us not allow this Satanic element in men to hinder us from realizing man! Let us release speech from its ban! Let us dare, despite all, to trust!" (1994, p. 311).

As an act of trust, dialogue is a subversive act against any powers or principalities that would halt the creative exchange by force or by oversimplification. It refuses to let dividing lines become firing lines. It refuses to let the hinderer have the final word. It patrols the dividing line, looking for someone with whom to speak. It continues to wage peace in the face of war. It rejects the option of despair and turns in quiet hope to the God of miracles.

For Christians, dialogue is the occasion for miracles. In dialogue, God's Spirit is able to bring forth healing, grace, growth, and reconciliation between two groups in ways not humanly orchestrated. We discover that God's Spirit is present among us, transforming the heat of our conflict into more illuminating light.

Allowing God to Work All Things for Good

The battles between Christians today are a major part of our collective story. We can chart their history and debate their causes, we can know that the level of division is not the will of God, but the fact that the church is divided and conflicted remains a given. The questions then become, What shall we do with this reality? Can anything good come out of this conflict?

Dialogue is a way to subject our lives and our world views to God's ways. As we bring our various perspectives to dialogue, there is the rich possibility that we may discover dimensions of the gospel message—deeper truths, more profound applications, greater wonders—that would have been undiscovered were it not for our many conflicts. If wars between nations could serve as the catalyst for important discoveries in medicine, communication, and engineering, then surely the God who "works all things for good" (Romans 8:28) is able to use the competing convictions of the church's culture war to bring important spiritual discoveries to light through the power of the Holy Spirit. As Pope John Paul II said, "For human knowledge and human action a certain dialectic is present. Didn't the Holy Spirit, in His divine 'condescendence,' take this into consideration? It is necessary for humanity to achieve unity through plurality, to learn to come together in the one Church, even while presenting a plurality of ways of thinking and acting, of cultures and civilizations" (quoted in Lefebure, 1995, p.176).

Figure 9.1.

Dialogue finds its voice through hope in God, whose word created this world out of the chaos, who defies human categories of order and logic, and who continues to place the treasure of his Spirit in clay jars (II Corinthians 4:7). It may turn out to be that this God is best understood in the coming together of seemingly conflicting convictions.

For this reason, I find the interlocking drawing of two faces in profile and the chalice (see Figure 9.1) to be an appropriate image for Christian dialogue. The drawing shows two people confronting each other, as if in a conflict. The chalice reminds us of the Cup of communion uniting all Christians. In dialogue, we are invited to see both realities, the faces and the Cup. When brought together, these two realities merge and transform into something different— a new symbol—wherein that which separates us is informed by that which unites us.

Lord, let it be!

Resource A: Organizations
That Facilitate Dialogue

Religious Organizations

Alban Institute
Suite 433 N, 4550 Montgomery Ave.
Bethesda, MD 20814–3341
800–486–1318
Alban Institute is an ecumenical organization that studies and promotes church life. Among its offerings, Alban provides consultants and original resources for churches and church agencies in need of conflict analysis and dispute mediation. Alban is well-known and respected for its work. (See Leas in Resource B.)

Mennonite Conciliation Services
Box 500
Akron, PA 17501
717–859–3889
This arm of the Mennonite Church makes its experiences in peace-making available to others through consultations, training, interventions, and printed resources, including a newsletter, *Conciliation Quarterly,* and a training manual (see Stutzman and Schrock-Shenk in Resource B). This organization is an excellent resource for the church in its culture war.

National Conference (formerly National Conference of Christians
and Jews)
71 Fifth Ave., Suite 1100
New York, NY 10003
800–352–6225
National Conference is a human relations organization dedicated
to fighting bias, bigotry, and racism in America. It promotes understanding and respect among all races, religions, and cultures through
advocacy, conflict resolution, and education. This organization has
a history of bringing groups together for dialogue.

Secular Organizations

Common Ground Network for Life and Choice
1601 Connecticut Ave., N.W. Suite 200
Washington, DC 20009
202–265–4300
A project of Search for Common Ground, CGN's approach to conflict emphasizes areas of intersection, or common ground, rather
than areas of difference. Initially focused on the abortion conflict,
CGN now addresses other conflicts as well. CGN offers consultation, planning, facilitation of dialogue for workshops and groups,
lectures and discussions about dialogue, training of small group facilitators, and printed resources.

Dialogue Group
23010 Lake Forest Dr. #342
Laguna Hills, CA 92653
310–822–4111
This organization does research, development, and facilitation of
dialogue based on the work of David Bohm, which presents dialogue
as not only a technique for communication, but also a new way of

thinking and relating to others. Dialogue Group promotes a philosophical analysis of the nature of dialogue; for example, one of its brochures defines dialogue this way: "Dialogue is a communication process aligned with the quantum and holographic nature of the universe and with chaos and complexity theory." The group offers beginning and advanced week-long conferences, tapes, and printed materials.

Food For Thought Gatherings
P.O. Box 2033
Colorado Springs, CO 80901–2033
719–634–0005
Internet: http://www.foodforthought.org
Begun in 1994 to address the tension and cultural division in Colorado Springs over Left-Right issues, this group facilitates face-to-face communication among people with differing beliefs and backgrounds through informal meals attended by eight to twelve participants along with a volunteer facilitator. Their success has been celebrated nationally.

Listening Project: Rural Southern Voices for Peace
1898 Hannah Branch Rd.
Burnsville, NC 28714
704–675–5933
e-mail: rsvp@igc.apc.org
Listening Project uses a method for beginning conversations in situations of conflict. People are trained to conduct thirty-minute to one-hour interviews with people on opposite sides of an issue through door-to-door surveys in which interviewees articulate their hopes and fears, rather than focusing on differences and prejudices. Interview results are used to develop new strategies that include everyone's concerns and insights. Topics have included race, abortion, and homosexuality.

Polarity Management Associates
4650 N. Breton Court SE
Grand Rapids, MI 49508
616–698–0271
e-mail: bjohnson@polaritymanagement.com
Internet: http://www.polaritymanagement.com
This organization offers a variety of consultations, customized assessments, and training for implementing the concepts of Polarity Management to organizations. The group has developed many valuable new insights since the important 1992 book on the subject (see Resource B).

Public Conversation Project
46 Kondazian St.
Watertown, MA 02172
617–923–1216
fax: 617–923–2757
e-mail:thepcpteam@aol.com
This group is an action-research project that seeks to develop models for dialogue facilitation on divisive political issues. It offers resource people to facilitate local dialogue initiatives, and it offers training on dialogue facilitation.

Study Circles Resource Center
P.O. Box 203
Pomfret, CT 06258
860-928-2616
Fax: 860-928-3713
e-mail: scrc@neca.com
The Study Circles Resource Center (SCRC) helps communities use study circles—small, democratic, highly participatory discussions— to involve large numbers of citizens in public dialogue and problem solving on critical social and political issues. Through this process, citizens gain "ownership" of issues and begin to see how they can effect change in their communities.

SCRC staff members work with community leaders at every stage of creating a grass-roots, community-wide study circle program: helping organizers network between communities; working to develop strong coalitions within communities; advising on material development; and writing letters of support for funding propsals. SCRC publishes and distributes discussion guides on issues such as race relations, crime and violence, education, American diversity, youth issues, and immigration, and produces a quarterly newsletter. Contact SCRC for information on these topical issue guides, "how-to" publications, and organizing and networking assistance.

Resource B: Selected Publications on Dialogue

Gerzon, Mark. *A House Divided*. New York: Putnam Books, 1996. (327 pages)
An analysis of the divisions that turn the United States into the "Divided States of America." The author contends that the competing views of what is good for the country threaten to undo us, despite the fact that each view has an important contribution to make to society. The nature of these competing views and the solutions offered have obvious parallels within the church's culture war. The book includes an excellent list of suggestions for transcending our nation's divisions as well as a thorough list of resources.

Halverstadt, Hugh F. *Managing Church Conflict*. Louisville, Ky.: Westminster/John Knox Press, 1991. (223 pages)
A brilliant exploration of conflict within the Christian community. Skilled in theology, ethics, and organizational systems, Halverstadt has helped churches deal creatively with conflicts for over twenty years. The book is somewhat complicated, with complex charts and graphs, but is an exceptional resource for serious students of conflict and dialogue.

Haynes, Charles C. ed. *Finding Common Ground*. Nashville, Tenn: The Freedom Forum First Amendment Center, 1994. (approximately 200 pages) (Contact the Freedom Forum at 615–321–9588).

A guide for civil discussion of the validity of teaching religion in a public-education setting. The guide aids people of differing church-state convictions to dialogue in a way that discovers common ground on which they can negotiate their differences in a productive manner. The book offers tips for discussing divisive issues; a reasoned history of the issue of religion and education; and a chapter on major issues that face local communities today, including religious holidays, equal access to use of school property by religious groups, religious expression in schools, and character-building education. Although focused on the church-state issue and the First Amendment of the Constitution, this guide provides a framework applicable to other church culture-war issues.

Jacksteit, Mary, and Kaufmann, Adrienne. *Finding Common Ground in the Abortion Conflict: A Manual.* Washington, D.C.: The Common Ground Network for Life and Choice, 1995. (96 pages)
An excellent primer for bringing people in conflict together for dialogue and work, this book includes schedules, sample letters, and follow-up actions.

Johnson, Barry. *Polarity Management.* Amherst, Mass.: HRD Press, 1992. (267 pages)
The primer for Polarity Management thinking, which offers an important new way to frame the issues dividing the church today.

Killmer, Richard J., and Lisherness, Sara P. *Suggestions for Using "Seeking to be Faithful Together: Guidelines for Presbyterians During Times of Disagreement."* Louisville, Ky.: Presbyterian Peacemaking Program, 100 Witherspoon St., 40202–1396, n.d. (41 pages)
A training manual that covers eight sessions to equip laypeople for the work of dialogue. It offers a well-packaged program for a church that wants a primer on exploring the nature of dialogue. The study is based on a 1992 Presbyterian Church (U.S.) document titled "Seeking to be Faithful Together."

Leas, Speed. *Moving Your Church Through Conflict*. An Alban Institute Publication (see "Alban Institute" in "Religious Organizations," Resource A), 1985. (84 pages)
An excellent framework for understanding conflicts among people of faith. Practical, tested, and usable, this book explores levels of conflict (a helpful insight) and possible strategies for each level, information gathering, strategies with individuals and tiny minorities, and the role of a consultant.

Mouw, Richard J. *Uncommon Decency: Christian Civility in an Uncivil World*. Downers Grove, Ill.: Intervarsity Press, 1992. (173 pages)
A folksy call from a widely respected evangelical leader encouraging the evangelical church to balance its faith convictions with gentleness and grace for opponents. Mouw shows that a spirit of openness and civility toward opponents is not compromising the gospel, but rather a faithful living out of obedience to Christ.

The National Conference, ed. "The Process of Dialogue," unpublished paper, April 1986. (See "National Conference" in "Religious Organizations," Resource A.)
Includes chapters on models for explaining the purpose and scope of dialogue to lay participants; a set of guidelines for group leadership; and an eight-page bibliography of materials (published prior to the early 1980s) on conflict management and other fields associated with dialogue.

New Mexico Conference of Churches. "A Protocol for Mediating Ethical/Moral Differences Within the Ecumenical Covenant of the New Mexico Conference of Churches." 124 Hermosa St. SE, Albuquerque, N. Mex. 87108–2610, adopted October 1987.
505–255–1509
fax: 505–256–0071

One group's attempt to articulate a way to live together amidst the diversity and conflict of church culture-war issues.

Perspectives. Winter 1996.
A journal of the McCormick Theological Seminary, this volume includes essays on how Presbyterians wrestle with the question of sexual orientation and ordination. See especially Hugh Halverstadt's excellent article on dialogue, "A Question of Continuing to Live Together."

Presbyterian Peacemaking Program. *Dealing with Conflict in the Congregation*. 100 Witherspoon St., Louisville, Ky. 40202–1396, n.d. (17 pages)
Four sessions to prepare congregations, especially leaders, to deal creatively with conflict. This booklet, published in the mid–1980s, is a concise work for congregations that want to explore the faith resources that affect conflict. A good one-page bibliography of materials written prior to the 1980s—most are still available.

Purdy, John C. *Behold, the New Has Come: Peacemaking in Corinthians*. Presbyterian Peacemaking Program, 100 Witherspoon St., Louisville, Ky. 40202–1396, n.d.
A five-session study of I and II Corinthians to help participants see that conflict is inevitable but potentially damaging if not handled effectively. The book explores Paul's suggestions for dealing with conflict. It is a hopeful study that trusts God's power to heal brokenness.

Rogers, Jack. *Claiming the Center*. Louisville, Ky.: Westminster/ John Knox Press, 1995. (222 pages)
An analysis of the culture war within the Presbyterian church that explores the various theological world views found within the battle (separatism, election, revivalism, common sense, moralism, and millenialism). Rogers advocates for the center amidst these positions as the proper place for the church.

Shriver, Donald W., Jr. *An Ethics For Enemies: Forgiveness in Politics.*
London: Oxford University Press, 1995.
An exploration of how nations or ethnic groups can learn to live
side-by-side after long struggles of violence. The book examines bib-
lical and historical work on forgiveness, justice, and reconciliation.
Shriver then takes three historic examples of long-term conflicts
(The U.S.-German relationship during and following World War
II; the U.S.-Japanese relationship prior to, during, and following
World War II; and the Civil Rights movement) to develop the
themes of forgiveness, memory, justice, vengeance, forbearance,
restitution, and reconciliation. The book examines conflict with an
understanding of the complexity of human social and political life as
well as the brutality and bitterness that can be so destructive to our
relationships.

Study Circles Resource Center, "Study Circles in Paired Congregations." 1995. (16 pages) (See "The Study Circles Resource Center"
in "Secular Organizations," Resource A.)
A primer for designing dialogue groups between churches. The
booklet also has a two-page annotated bibliography of dialogue-
related resources not contained in this appendix.

Stutzman, Jim, and Schrock-Shenk, Carolyn, eds. (3rd ed.) *Mediation and Facilitation Training Manuel.* Akron, Pa.: Mennonite Conciliation Service, 1995. (310 pages) (See "Mennonite Conciliation
Services" in "Religious Organizations," Resource A.)
Practical resources, articles, bibliographies, and methodology compiled by a Christian group that has been studying and practicing
nonviolent, justice-oriented interaction for centuries. An invaluable resource for any serious participant in dialogue.

Watts, Richard G. *How Should Congregations Talk About Tough
Issues?* Presbyterian Peacemaking Program, 100 Witherspoon St.,
Louisville, Ky., 40202–1396, 1987.

A concise, manageable, six-session study guide to prepare congregations for dealing with conflict within the church. (A companion video is also available but is of little use.)

The Witness. 77: April 1994.
This volume of the journal of the Episcopal church was dedicated to the subject of dialogue, with articles by Walter Brueggemann, Ched Myers, and others.

Video Resources

Common Ground Network. "What's the Common Ground on Abortion?" August 1994. (See "Common Ground Network for Life and Choice" in "Secular Organizations," Resource A.) (28 minutes)
A live-audience talk show with two abortion adversaries discussing how they sought common ground despite their differences.

Friendship Press, "Seeking The Common Good." P.O. Box 37844, Cincinnati, Ohio, 45222–0844. (30 minutes.)
A presentation of the struggle to determine the common good in two different communities faced with conflict—one in Barbour County, West Virginia, where the conflict is over a landfill site, the other in Westchester County, New York, where the issue is putting a homeless shelter in the community. Comments by three ethicists are included. This video is a good way to introduce the need for resources for dialogue. Not church-oriented.

Public Affairs Television, "Bill Moyer's Journal: The New Holy War." 356 West 58th St., New York, N.Y., 10019, November 19, 1993.
Chronicles the division over Amendment 2, on homosexuality, in Colorado Springs, CO. The video shows both sides of the issues and attempts to bring the groups together in dialogue.

The Synod of Lakes and Prairies, Presbyterian Church (U.S.), "Coping with Conflict." 8012 Cedar Ave. South, Bloomington, Minn., 55425–1210, 1988. (Approximately 45 minutes)

A two-video set for church leaders that explores conflict, its inevitability, early warning signs, how to manage conflict, channeling conflict's energy, and knowing when to call for help. The follow-up tape examines each of the five levels of conflict and how to respond to them. An excellent resource packet and discussion guide comes with the video.

Works Cited

Aesop, "The Mice in Council." In *Aesop's Fables*. New York: Grosset and Dunlap, 1947.

Ackerman, B. *Social Justice in the Liberal State*. New Haven: Yale University Press, 1980.

Anderson, R., Cissna, K. N., and Arnett, R. C. (eds.). *The Reach of Dialogue: Confirmation, Voice, and Community*. Cresskill, N.J.: Hampton Press, 1994.

Barclay, W. *The Gospel of John*. Vol. 2. Philadelphia: Westminster Press, 1955.

Becker, C., and others. "From Stuck Debate to New Conversation on Controversial Issues: A Report from the Public Conversation Project." *Journal of Feminist Family Therapy*, 1995, 7, 143–163.

Bennett, W. "Stop Bashing the Christian Right." *Christianity Today*, 1994, 38, 10.

Bohm, D. "Transforming the Culture Through Dialogue." *Utne Reader*, Mar./Apr. 1991, pp. 82.

———. *Unfolding Meaning*. Loveland, Colo.: Foundation House, 1985.

Brown, J. "Dialogue: Capacities and Stories." In S. Chawla and J. Renesch (eds.), *Learning Organizations*. Portland, Oreg.: Productivity Press, 1995.

Brueggemann, W. "Disputing the Hegemony in God and in Us." *The Witness*, 1994, 77, 16–19.

Buber, M. *Between Man and Man*. New York: Macmillan, 1965.

———. "Genuine Dialogue and the Possibilities of Peace." In R. Anderson (ed.), *The Reach of Dialogue*. Cresskill, N.J.: Hampton Press, 1994.

Carter, S. L. *(integrity)*. New York: HarperCollins, 1996.

Chasin, R., and Herzig, M. "Creating Systemic Interventions for the Sociopolitical Arena." In B. B. Gould and D. H. DeMuth (eds.), *The Global Family Therapist: Integrating the Personal, Professional, and Political*. Needham Heights, Mass.: Allyn & Bacon, 1994.

Chasin, R., and others. "From Diatribe to Dialogue on Divisive Public Issues: Approaches Drawn from Family Therapy." *Mediation Quarterly*, 1996, *13*, 323.

Cobb, J. B., Jr. "Being a Transformationist in a Pluralistic World." *The Christian Century*, 1994, *111*, 23.

"The Cry for Renewal." Washington, D.C., May 29, 1995.

Dobson, J. "Why I Use 'Fighting Words.'" *Christianity Today*, 1995, *39* (7), 27–30.

Eck, D. *Encountering God*. Boston: Beacon Press, 1993.

"'Economic Hardball' Won in NIV Controversy, Critic Says." *Western Recorder*, 1998, *172*, p. 12.

Fackre, G. "An Altar Call for Evangelicals." *The Christian Century*, Nov. 17–24, 1993, 1169.

Fisher, R. and Ury W., *Getting To Yes: Negotiating Agreement Without Giving In*. Boston: Houghton Mifflin, 1981.

Gaede, B. (ed.). *Congregations Talking About Homosexuality*. Bethesda, Md. Alban Institute, 1998.

Graff, G. *Beyond the Culture Wars*. New York: Norton, 1992.

Gunderson, G. R. "Tools for Change." In *The Challenges of Faith and Health*. The Report of the National Conference of the Interfaith Health Program, The Carter Center, n.d.

Howe, R. *The Miracle of Dialogue*. New York: Seabury Press, 1963.

———. "Dialogue Reconsidered." *Christian Ministry*, 1972, *3*, 6–9.

Hunter, J. D. *Culture Wars*. New York: HarperCollins, 1991.

———. *Before the Shooting Begins*. New York: Free Press, 1994.

Hunter, J. D., and Guinness, O. *Articles of Faith, Articles of Peace: The Religious Liberty Clauses and the American Public Philosophy*. Washington, D.C.: Brookings Institution, 1990.

Johnson, B. *Polarity Management*. Amherst, Mass.: HRD Press, 1992.

Kelly, D. M., and Olson, B. E. *The Meaning and Conduct of Dialogue*. The National Conference of Christians and Jews New York, n.d.

Leas, S. B. *Leadership and Conflict*. Nashville: Abingdon Press, 1982.

Lefebure, L. D. "John Paul II: The Philosopher Pope." *Christian Century*, 1995, *112*, 170–176.

Marty, M. E. "Heaping It On." *Christian Century*, 1995, *112*, 999.

———. "A Modest Master." *Dallas Morning News*, Apr. 29, 1995b, p. 3G.

Mathewes-Green, F. "Pro-Life, Pro-Choice: Can We Talk?" *Christian Century*, 1996, *113*, 12–15.

———. "Wanted: A New Pro-Life Strategy." *Christianity Today*, 1998, *42*, 27–30.

Mauldin, D. C. "Southern Baptists Together: The Whitsitt Experiment." *Christian Century*, 1995, *112*, 513–515.

McKenny, G. P. "From Consensus to Consent." *Soundings*, 1991, *74*, 427–457.

Mouw, R. *Uncommon Decency: Christian Civility in an Uncivil World*. Downers Grove, Ill.: Intervarsity Press, 1992.

Muck, T. C. "The New Testament Case for Interreligious Dialogue." *Insights*, 1995, *110*, 7–22.

Neuhaus, R. J. *Naked Public Square*. Grand Rapids, Mich.: Wm. B. Eerdmans, 1984.

Newbigin, L. The Gospel in a Pluralist Society. Grand Rapids, Mich.: Wm. B. Eerdmans, 1989.

Peck, M. S. *The Road Less Traveled*. New York: Simon & Schuster, 1978.

Pieterse, H. "A Dialogical Theory of Communication from a Practical Theological Perspective." *Evangelical Quarterly*, 1990, *62*, 223–240.

Public Conversation Project. *Dialogues on Abortion: A Field Manual*. (forthcoming)

Rogers, J. *Claiming the Center*. Louisville: Westminster John Knox Press, 1995.

Rokeach, M. *The Open and Closed Mind*. New York: Basic Books, 1960.

———. *Beliefs, Attitudes, and Values*. San Francisco: Jossey-Bass, 1968.

Senge, P. M. *The Fifth Discipline*. New York: Doubleday/Currency, 1990.

Senge, P. M., and others. *The Fifth Discipline Fieldbook*. New York: Doubleday, 1994.

Sine T. *Cease Fire: Searching for Sanity in America's Culture Wars*. Grand Rapids, Mich.: Wm. B. Eerdmans, 1995.

Sire, J. W. "Guinness' New Covenant for America." *Christianity Today*, 1993, *39*, 49–51.

Skillen, J. "Public Justice and True Tolerance". In R. Neuhaus and M. Cromartie (eds.), *Piety and Politics*. Washington, D.C.: Ethics and Public Policy Center, 1987.

Stassen, G. *Journey into Peacemaking*. Memphis: Brotherhood Commission, 1983.

Stutzman, J., and Schrock-Shenk, C. (eds.). *Mediation and Facilitation Training Manual* (3rd ed.). Akron, Pa.: Mennonite Conciliation Service, 1995.

Swidler, L. "The Dialogue Decalogue." *Journal of Ecumenical Studies*, *20*, 1983. (Also available in brochure form.)

Taylor, D. *The Myth of Certainty*. Grand Rapids, Mich.: Zondervan, 1992.

Teurfs, L. "Finding a Shared Meaning: Reflections on Dialogue." *Seeds of Unfolding*. 1994, Vol. XI, (1), 4–10.

Tracy, D. *Plurality and Ambiguity*. San Francisco: Harper & Row, 1987.

Wallis, J. *The Soul of Politics*. New York: New Press, 1994.

Williams, R. H. "Is America in a Culture War? Yes—No—Sort Of." *Christian Century*, 1997, *114*, 1038–1043.

Woodbridge, J. D. "Culture War Casualties." *Christianity Today*, 1995, *39*, 20–26.

Wuthnow, R. *The Struggle for America's Soul*. Grand Rapids, Mich.: Wm. B. Eerdmans, 1989.

Yoder, J. H. *Body Politics: Five Practices of the Christian Community Before the Watching World*. Nashville: Discipleship Resources, 1992.

Index